Discovering God's Will
for Your Life

Other Crossway Books by Ray Pritchard

The Road Best Traveled
Man of Honor
What a Christian Believes

DISCOVERING GOD'S WILL FOR YOUR LIFE

RAY PRITCHARD

CROSSWAY BOOKS

A DIVISION OF
GOOD NEWS PUBLISHERS
WHEATON, ILLINOIS

Discovering God's Will for Your Life

Adapted from part of *The Road Best Traveled*, copyright © 1995 by Ray Pritchard. Published by Crossway Books.

Copyright © 2004 by Ray Pritchard

Published by Crossway Books
    A division of Good News Publishers
    1300 Crescent Street
    Wheaton, Illinois 60187

Cover design: Josh Dennis

Cover photo: Photonica

First printing, 2004

Printed in the United States of America

Library of Congress Cataloging-in-Publication Data
Pritchard, Ray, 1952-
   Discovering God's will for your life / Ray Pritchard.
     p. cm.
    ISBN 1-58134-611-5 (alk. paper)
    1. Christian life. 2. God—Will. I. Title.
BV4509.5.P76   2004
248.4—dc22   2004007462

CH		13	12	11	10	09	08	07	06	05	04
15	14	13	12	11	10	9	8	7	6	5	4	3	2	1

To
CHRISTINE STOUT and MORGAN WILLIAMS
You became part of our family

CONTENTS

ACKNOWLEDGMENTS

After hearing me preach on God's will, Brian Ondracek told me that I should write a book. Lane Dennis and Len Goss invited me to write the manuscript that became *The Road Best Traveled*. Ten years later Marvin Padgett asked me to do the revision that resulted in *Discovering God's Will for Your Life*. Ted Griffin did his usual superb job of editing—both of the original manuscript and the revision a decade later. The congregation of Calvary Memorial Church of Oak Park, Illinois, listens patiently to my sermons every Sunday. I depend upon their prayers. I am grateful to my wife Marlene and to our three boys—Josh, Mark, and Nick—for their love and constant encouragement.

INTRODUCTION

This is a book I never intended to write. I say that because it is based on a series of sermons I never intended to preach. It happened like this. Early one January I laid out my preaching plans for the year, and they didn't include preaching on God's will. But that began to change somewhere along the way, perhaps about March or April. Almost every day I found myself talking with people who sought advice about major decisions they were facing. A job change . . . a move across the country . . . where to go to college . . . the call to foreign missions . . . hiring new employees . . . buying a new home . . . marriage, divorce, and remarriage . . . whether or not to have more children.

Then there were the hard questions: "Why did my father get cancer?" "How can I be 100 percent certain of God's will?" "Does God speak to us through dreams and visions today?" "Is it wrong to go to R-rated movies?" "Should I put out a fleece?" The list seemed to have no end.

One day in July I began jotting notes on the will of God. Out flowed ideas, quotes, comments made to me over the years, stories of people searching for direction, crucial Scriptures, pressing questions, areas of common confusion, and popular misunderstandings. On and on I wrote, page after page, surprising myself by the sheer volume I generated in only two hours.

But I still didn't have a sermon series. How would I take that mass of uncongealed study and bring order from the chaos? I left the matter alone for a week or so, coming back to it during my vacation in August. We spent the first days on a lake in southern Michigan. Then we traveled north to the Upper Peninsula, to Sault St. Marie, and west to Wisconsin where we spent one rainy night in Green Bay. I wrote notes as we traveled, pulling my scattered thoughts together as we motored through one small town after another. We arrived back in Oak Park for one day, washed our clothes, and set out for the Illinois State Fair in Springfield. Several days later we pushed farther south to visit my younger brother in Mississippi who graciously allowed us the free run of his camp. While the boys went swimming in the lake, I jotted down more notes. Next we traveled to Alabama to visit my older brother, then turned north to make our way back to Chicago. More notes, thoughts, and ideas flowed from my pen onto paper as we made our way through Bluegrass Country into Indiana.

By the time we got home the series had come together in my mind. Several weeks later I preached the first sermon: "Does God Still Guide?" The response was so encouraging that I knew this was what God had wanted all along. True preaching is always a two-way conversation between the pulpit and the pew. The preacher listens, then speaks, then listens again. What you are about to read is more than the sermons I preached. More than ten years have passed since I finished that series and since I wrote the first edition of this book. In the years since then, I have continued to listen to the voices of many people as they told of their journeys with the Lord, and I have grown in my own understanding of God's will. I thought you ought to know the background because this book was born out of the real-life questions of people standing at the crossroads of life. There is nothing theoretical in the following pages. Everything here was forged on the anvil of human experience.

That's why this book is filled with stories. Some of them have happy endings; some don't. Many of them tell of decisions made, but the final result is not yet known. As you read this book, please take time to consider the questions at the end of each chapter. Don't skip them. They are designed to help you grapple with the major concepts and then apply them to your own life.

After writing this book, I am more convinced than ever that you *can* discover God's will for your life. More than that, I am fully persuaded that if you want to do God's will, you will do it. If that sounds exciting, turn the page, and let's get started.

1

Does God Still Guide?

The year was 1915, and America was inching toward World War I. In Liverpool, England, a young man decided to return to New Hampshire while he still had the chance. As he prepared to leave England, he composed a poem that he later insisted had been simply a gentle joke written for a good friend. Yet that composition became one of the best-loved poems of the twentieth century.

> *Two roads diverged in a yellow wood,*
> *And sorry I could not travel both*
> *And be one traveler, long I stood*
> *And looked down one as far as I could*
> *To where it bent in the undergrowth;*
>
> *Then took the other, just as fair,*
> *And having perhaps the better claim,*
> *Because it was grassy and wanted wear;*
> *Though as for that the passing there*
> *Had worn them really about the same,*

And both that morning equally lay
In leaves no step had trodden black.
Oh, I kept the first for another day!
Yet knowing how way leads on to way,
I doubted if I should ever come back.

I shall be telling this with a sigh
Somewhere ages and ages hence:
Two roads diverged in a wood, and I—
I took the one less traveled by,
And that has made all the difference.

The poet was Robert Frost. His poem is known around the world as "The Road Not Taken." All of us have been there!

We have all come to a crossroads of life where two roads diverged, one winding off to the left, the other disappearing in the distance to the right. We stood at the fork in the road and wondered, *Should I go this way or should I go that way?*

OUR DECISIONS MAKE US

Our decisions really do matter. *We make our decisions, and our decisions turn around and make us.* We face so many questions:

- Should I get married? If the answer is yes, should I marry Joe or Jake? Should I marry Susan or Sally?
- Should I go to college? If the answer is yes, should I go to Alabama or Penn State or UCLA?
- I've been offered a new job. It's a good one. But I already have a good job. Should I take the new position? Or should I hold on to what I have?
- We have two children. We're thinking about having a third. Should we have another one? Should we think about adopting?
- Is God calling me to the mission field? How can I be

sure? Three mission boards are interested in me. How
do I know which one to choose?

YOU CAN'T GO BACK

We make our decisions, and our decisions turn around and make
us. If you go to UCLA, you won't go to Alabama or Penn State
or anywhere else—at least not this year. Even if you think you
might transfer next year, that won't be the same as going there this
year. You can major in biology or business administration—you
can even take a double major if you like; but whichever path you
take, you can't go back and be an eighteen-year-old college fresh-
man again. And if you marry Sue instead of Barbara, that one
decision will stay with you—for better or for worse—for the rest
of your life. Even if for some reason you get a divorce that ends
your marriage, you'll live with the consequences forever.

Sometimes the slightest decisions, made in haste and without
much thought, turn out to have the greatest impact. Years ago
while pastoring a church in the Los Angeles area, a letter arrived
one day asking if I would consider moving to Texas to become
the first pastor of a new church in a Dallas suburb. I had never
heard of the church or the man who signed the letter. That particular day I was not in the mood to consider moving anywhere.
Nothing in the letter sounded particularly inviting or intriguing.
In fact, I couldn't think of a single reason to get excited about
moving to Texas. But what should I do about the invitation? I had
to respond one way or the other. As I stood by my desk thinking
about it, the envelope in my hand, I tried to decide whether to
throw it away or toss it on my desk. For some reason that I still
don't fully understand, I tossed the envelope on my desk.

From that rather haphazard, spur-of-the-moment decision
came a major redirection of my life. One thing led to another, and
I ended up as a pastor for five and a half very eventful years in

Garland, Texas. I didn't see it then, and I couldn't have known how important that casual decision was. I'm sure I didn't pray about whether to toss the envelope in the trash or on my desk. Looking back on it, I had no sense that I was standing at a crossroads. Two roads diverged in a yellow wood that afternoon in California, and by choosing not to throw away an unexpected letter, I unknowingly chose the road "less traveled."

THE ROMANCE OF GOD'S WILL

Most of us have similar stories. Just as a massive ship is guided by a tiny rudder, our lives often turn on small decisions and unexpected events. An unplanned phone call, a "chance" conversation in the hallway, a friend we "happen" to meet in a restaurant, a fragment of a remembered dream, a book we meant to return but didn't, the dry cleaning we forgot to pick up, a newspaper story that led to an idea that became a dissertation topic that earned a degree that opened a door to a job in another country. It happens all the time.

Life *is* unpredictable. That's the romance of trying to discover God's will for your life. Does the word *romance* sound unusual to you in connection with God's will? It shouldn't. As we move on together through the chapters of this book, we'll discover that *knowing God's will is really all about knowing God.* But knowing God can never be reduced to a mechanical formula, any more than the marriage between a man and a woman can be reduced to Three Steps or Four Keys or Five Rules. Since knowing God is central to knowing his will, what you will find are biblical stories that, like pieces of a puzzle, fit together to give us a better understanding of what it means to know God personally. Out of those stories we will draw principles that show us how God's will is discovered in the outworking of the ordinary affairs of life.

MORE THAN A BIRTHDAY CAKE

I can't say that I've always looked at God's will this way. Years ago I looked at the subject in a rather mechanical fashion—"Do these three things and you'll discover God's will." Unfortunately, the only thing I discovered was that the "three things" don't always work as advertised. The "three things" are indeed helpful, and even essential, just as remembering your spouse's birthday is essential to a healthy marriage. But marriage is more than a birthday cake, and knowing God's will is more than having a quiet time in the morning.

What, then, is this book all about? I propose to share the theme of this book in one sentence. If you want to know what *Discovering God's Will for Your Life* is all about, here it is: *God wants you to know his will more than you want to know it, and therefore he takes personal responsibility to see that you discover it.* Knowing God's will is ultimately God's problem, not yours. The sooner you realize that, the happier you will be. Too many people agonize over God's will as if God were playing a cosmic game of hide-and-seek. The entire Bible teaches us the opposite, that our God seeks us. He continually takes the initiative to reveal himself to us. Therefore, knowing God's will is simply a subsection of the larger question of knowing God personally.

That's the whole book in a nutshell. If you're looking for a quick-fix approach, this is probably not the book for you. But if you would like to know God better, *and through knowing God learn more about knowing his will*, read on.

WHAT THIS BOOK CAN'T DO

One disclaimer: If you are currently in the yellow wood standing at the crossroads as you read these words, and if you are hoping that this book will tell you which road to take, you will probably be disappointed. Nothing in these pages will make your decisions for you. You'll still have to choose between UCLA and Florida State or between moving to South Carolina or staying in Oregon. If you're wondering whether to marry Joe or Harry, you'll have to decide that for yourself. No book written by mortal man can make your choices for you.

But as you move through these chapters, I can promise you some new insights into who God is and how he reveals himself to his children. I'm sure that you'll approach your decisions with more confidence and less fear once you discover how much God wants you to know his will. Nothing is more comforting to the child of God than knowing that amid the confusion of everyday life God is slowly leading him or her along the path of his will. In fact, he is working in and through your decisions (and often in spite of your decisions) to see that his will is actually done in your life.

A PERSONAL WORD

I have a personal interest in this subject because I have agonized over the will of God. Recently I took a look back over the fifty-one years of my life. *I realized that who I am today is the result of all the decisions I have made until now.* I am the result of hundreds and thousands of decisions, many of which did not seem very important at the time. I have already mentioned tossing the envelope from Texas on my desk instead of in the trash can. But there were many others.

- When I was in the fourth grade my friend Tommy Thompson joined the band. I joined soon after he did, learned how to play the trombone, and saved up money to go to the Cotton Carnival in Memphis, Tennessee, when I was about thirteen years old. There I visited a radio station and met a disc jockey who showed me the news as it came off the AP wire. When he gave me a handful of yellow sheets with news reports on them, I was so excited I could hardly sleep that night.

• When I was in the seventh grade I began stopping by Ira's Gift and Book Shop. Every week Ira Schnell gave me a copy of a Christian magazine. It was the first place I ever saw the Gospel of Jesus Christ clearly set forth in print.

• When I was a senior in high school, I decided to enter the Junior Civitan Public Speaking Competition, won the local contest, and went on to the regional competition.

• When I graduated from high school I was offered a college scholarship, and without much thought I said no because it wasn't the right place for me.

• Three years later I took a deep breath and said hi to that cute girl who was the secretary of the music department in the college that I attended.

• The year after my father died and my faith had taken a major hit, I chose—almost by throwing a dart at a piece of paper—to go to Paraguay for a summer missions trip that turned my life and our marriage completely around.

From one decision came a love of music and journalism, from another the realization that yes, I could stand and speak well before an audience, from yet another a courtship that led to marriage, from another a major moment of personal renewal.

Over the years I have made thousands of decisions, many of which seemed trivial at the time. But taken together they have made me exactly who I am today. The same is true for all of us. *We make our decisions, and then our decisions turn around and make us.*

THE CRUCIAL QUESTION

There are many different ways to ask this question. You could ask: How can I, a mere mortal, ever discover what Almighty God wants me to do? Or you might wonder, how can I bring God into the reality of my daily life? Or you could go right to the bottom line: Where is God when I have to make a really tough decision? Or you could ask it this way: Does God still guide? In the moments of life when you have to make a tough decision, when you are in the woods with the two roads diverging in front of you, can you count on God to help you?

Some years ago when I was in a desperate moment of my own life, I stumbled across Psalm 48:14, "This is God, our God forever and ever. He will guide us forever." I had lost my job and had no prospects on the horizon. I had a wife, three children, and a mortgage payment to make. When I desperately needed to know what God wanted me to do, this verse was precious to me. It sustained me in some dark moments when I wondered if I would be able to take care of my family. Out of that crucible I discovered that God does indeed guide his children.

FOLLOW THAT CLOUD!

Many stories in the Bible illustrate this truth. But few episodes grip the imagination like the story of the cloud and the pillar of fire that led God's people through the wilderness. The nation of Israel was leaving the land of Egypt. After they crossed the Red Sea, they would go to Mount Sinai, and eventually they would come to the Promised Land. In the process of leaving the safety and security of Egypt, something amazing happened. Exodus 13:20-22 tells the story:

> *And they moved on from Succoth and encamped at Etham, on the edge of the wilderness. And the LORD went before*

them by day in a pillar of cloud to lead them along the way, and by night in a pillar of fire to give them light, that they might travel by day and by night. The pillar of cloud by day and the pillar of fire by night did not depart from before the people.

The desert was behind them, the Red Sea was in front of them, and the Egyptians were closing fast from behind. Unable to go back to Egypt, trapped between water in front of them and the armies of Pharaoh to the rear, the people of God found themselves between the devil and the deep blue sea, you might say. Even if they somehow made it across the vast stretch of water, they faced an unknown future. As bad as Pharaoh had been, at least in Egypt they felt secure—they knew what to expect. But what would they do now that they were leaving their security behind them?

God answered their concern by sending them a moving pillar to guide them on their way. During the day the pillar was a visible cloud in the sky. During the night the cloud became a blazing pillar of fire that provided visible, unmistakable guidance twenty-four hours a day, seven days a week. All they had to do was follow the cloud and the fire and they would be safe.

Numbers 9:15-23 explains how the cloud and pillar of fire actually worked. The passage is a bit long, but I find it fascinating in its details:

On the day that the tabernacle was set up, the cloud covered the tabernacle, the tent of the testimony. And at evening it was over the tabernacle like the appearance of fire until morning. So it was always: the cloud covered it by day and the appearance of fire by night. And whenever the cloud lifted from over the tent, after that the people of Israel set out, and in the place where the cloud settled down, there the people of Israel camped. At the command of the LORD the people of Israel set out, and at the command of the LORD they camped. As long as the cloud rested over the tabernacle, they remained in camp. Even when the cloud continued over the tabernacle many days, the people of Israel kept the charge of the LORD and did not set out. Sometimes the cloud was a few days over the tabernacle, and according to the command of the LORD they remained in camp; then according to the command of the LORD they set out. And sometimes the cloud remained from evening until morning. And when the cloud lifted in the morning, they set out, or if it continued for a day and a night, when the cloud lifted they set out. Whether it was two days, or a month, or a longer time, that the cloud continued over the tabernacle, abiding there, the people of Israel remained in camp and did not set out, but when it lifted they set out. At the command of the LORD they camped, and at the command of the LORD they set out. They kept the charge of the LORD, at the command of the LORD by Moses.

Using this story as a guide, I want to share with you four lessons from the cloud and the fire that explain to us something about how God guides his people.

Lesson #1:
God's guidance is revealed to us one step at a time

Numbers 9 makes this very clear. The cloud would lift, and they would go. As long as the cloud kept moving, they would follow. When it stopped, they would stop. Sometimes it would stop for a night and go on the next morning. Then it would stop for a few days, and they would stop for a few days. The Israelites never knew from moment to moment or day to day what the cloud was going to do next.

Many Christians trip over this very point because they want to see ten steps ahead before they will take the first step. But life doesn't work that way. God rarely shows you ten steps in advance. He normally leads you one step at a time. He will lead you a step, then he'll lead you another step, and then he'll lead you another step. After he's led you ten steps, you look back and say, "How did I get from there to here?" Then you realize it was just step by step by step.

Lesson #2:
God's guidance demands our obedience whether it makes sense to us or not

One day the cloud would just stop in the middle of the desert; so that's where the people of Israel set up camp. Ten days later it would suddenly begin to move again. Why? Why not ten weeks? Or ten months? Or why not just keep moving? No one—not even Moses—knew the answers to those questions. Many days it didn't make any sense at all.

God's guidance is often like that. *Sometimes God keeps you moving when you would rather stop.* That's happening to one of my close friends as I write these words. All his life he has lived in the Chicago area. His life is here, his children are happy here, his wife is from this area, he knows and understands Chicago. Several years ago he started a new job with a national firm headquartered in a major southern city. For a year he flew in and out of Chicago, visiting customers from coast to coast. As a reward for his good work, his company offered to make him president of a brand-new division. There was only one condition: He had to move to the home office. For months he agonized, prayed, sought godly counsel, waited for God to open other doors. At the same time he became an elder at our church, and he and his wife became leaders in our contemporary worship service. More than once I have heard him say, "I have no idea why God is doing this because I'd rather stay in Chicago." But in spite of all that, he is moving to a new state and entering a new culture, because for him and his family the cloud is moving on.

KEEP YOUR BAGS PACKED

Can you imagine what it was like to wander in the wilderness for forty years? Say, you're in year twenty-three—only seventeen more years to go! For the last fourteen years it seems like you've been moving in circles in the desert. Finally the cloud stops. You're somewhere south of Kadesh-Barnea, about a hundred miles from Zoar, twenty-seven miles from Hazeroth, and roughly three miles from the end of the world. They call this place "the Desert of Zin." It's hot, rocky, barren, dusty—not a sign of life for miles in any direction. But the cloud has finally stopped. So you start to set up camp. You get the tent up and find some rocks to make a temporary sheepfold. You think to yourself, *Well, it looks like we're going to be here for a while.* There's an oasis just over the next hill where you can get water. The next morning the cloud lifts. That makes you angry; so you look at the sky and have a conversation with the Lord: "What's going on? We just arrived. I just fed the sheep. I just put up the tent. What are you doing?" And the Lord says, "What I'm doing is moving. If you are going to follow me, you are going to have to move with me."

"LORD, WE'VE BEEN HERE LONG ENOUGH"

The other side is also true. *Sometimes the Lord says, "Stay" when we would rather be moving.* A friend wrote to say that she is struggling over this very point. Now that she and her husband have retired, they have plenty of time on their hands. Both of them would love to use their gifts in the Lord's work. But no opportunities have presented themselves. My friend wrote of "times when

God puts you (the empty vessel) back in the cupboard, clean, but doesn't use you to cook his soup. I know that our part is just to be there—ready for his use, but it's boring." Then she added these perceptive words: "Shame on me for saying I am bored with my Christian life. But—this restlessness, yet not being able to change anything—is hard!" She and her husband are ready to move on. Why is the cloud standing still?

I don't know the answer to that question. All I know is this: Sometimes God says, "Wait" when we would rather move. Chuck Swindoll calls waiting the hardest discipline in the Christian life. I agree. That is why the psalmist says, "Be still before the LORD and wait patiently for him" (Psalm 37:7).

Let this lesson soak into your soul: *God's guidance demands our obedience, even when it makes no sense to us.* Sometimes God moves when we want to stay. Sometimes God says, "Stay" when we would rather move on and get our life going again.

Lesson #3:
God's guidance changes its character according to the need of the moment

During the day when the Israelites needed to see a cloud, God provided a cloud; but at night when the cloud would be invisible, the cloud looked like fire. God had one way of showing himself to them during the day and another way of showing himself at night.

That leads me to this conclusion: *God's guidance is always there, but his various means of guiding us change from moment to moment.* Consider the implications of that statement. God is not obligated to lead you in the same way he leads somebody else. God is not obligated to deal with you today in the same way he dealt with you yesterday or the way he is going to deal with you tomorrow.

WHICH HOUSE SHOULD WE BUY?

That's an important principle to learn because so many of us have a very narrow view of God. We think that since God dealt with our best friend a certain way, he's therefore obligated to deal with us in the same way. "Lord, you answered her prayer that way. Now please do the same for me." God says, "No deal."

I've always admired (and perhaps slightly envied) those people who seem to have a direct connection with the Lord. When the time comes to make a major decision, they always seem to have an unusual experience, a startling answer to prayer, or an unexplainable "coincidence" that happens to them at just the right moment. In fact, some of my friends routinely expect such things to happen to them so that—from the outside at least—decision-making seems to come easily to them. Not so with me. I've discovered over the years that I tend to agonize over big decisions. Sometimes the moment comes when you just have to make up your mind. When I wrote the first edition of this book ten years ago, our family was in the midst of moving from one house to another. Let me repeat the story exactly as I wrote it a decade ago:

To be more specific, we've already sold our home and as of this moment don't know where we are going next. This happened because our home sold too fast—in eight days to be exact. The people who are buying our home made us an offer we couldn't refuse, but they also want to take possession in about five weeks. So for the last few days, we've been scrambling, hastily visiting every other available home in Oak Park, Illinois, in our price range. I can summarize what we've found very simply: nice houses but too expensive; nice houses but too far from where we want to live; nice houses but too small; or nice houses that need lots of work. (It's not hard for me to determine God's will regarding that last category since I'm not a handyman.) But we did find a handful of houses that met our criteria. In fact, the day before yesterday we settled on two houses.

Both are within our price range, and both could potentially meet our needs. One is a charming, eighty-year-old, three-story home. It's very typical of the homes in Oak Park. It offers lots of room and lots of possibilities for the future. The other is a much newer, ranch-style home in a very nice section of central Oak Park. How does one make a decision when both houses are appealing and good arguments could be made for either one? It is small comfort to say that you can't go wrong either way (which is true). We have to choose one or the other. Or we have to find another house and start the process all over again.

Yesterday as I walked from the church down to the real estate office to sign some papers, the thought hit me that no matter how much we discuss the matter or how many family discussions we have, there will always be some degree of uncertainty about our decision. In times past God has intervened to show us precisely what he wanted us to do. This time we are left to use our best judgment after spending time in prayer and in the Word and consulting many advisers (who tell us many different things).

Now let's jump a decade ahead and fast-forward to the present day. We ended up buying the ranch-style home in central Oak Park. It turned out to be a great place to raise our three boys. We have been very happy in every way. Once we made the decision, we never looked back. But now our boys are out of high school, and the youngest will soon graduate from college. My wife and I are now empty-nesters, and our home seems bigger than what we need. So we're in the market again. This time we're looking at townhomes, and we're thinking about moving to a community a few miles west of Oak Park so I can ride my bike on the local trails. A decade ago I didn't own a bike; now I ride thousands of miles each year. I've become such an avid rider that finding a home near the bike trails has become a priority.

That wasn't on the radar screen the last time we bought a home. Ten years ago we searched, waited, prayed, discussed, compared, negotiated, and sought the Lord's will. We never heard a voice from heaven or even had a strong inner sense of God's leading. Up until the very day we bought that ranch-style home, I had some doubts about the decision. Looking back, we made the right decision—no doubt about it. But I couldn't be certain in advance. To be fair about it, my wife liked the ranch-style home more than I did—she could see what it would become. She was right, and I'm glad we made that choice. Now a decade later we've come to the same crossroads, and it's not any easier. I simply repeat what I said ten years ago. God has promised to guide us, and he will keep his promise. And when the day comes, I'm likely to have the same uncertainty I had ten years ago, and my wife will probably be more persuaded than I am. That thought gives me enormous comfort because it means God's guidance does not depend on my personal understanding at any given moment. If we need to be in a townhome, that's where we'll end up. If the Lord wants us near a bike trail (as I fervently hope he does), he will lead us to the right home at the right time. Exactly how he will do that doesn't matter. It's enough to know that God doesn't abandon us even when we are confused and uncertain about the choices before us.

MANY WAYS, ONE VOICE

How does God guide his people? A thousand different ways. But no matter what form the guidance may take, it will always be 100 percent consistent with the Word of God, because God does not contradict himself. God's moment-by-moment leading comes through a variety of means. Sometimes through the advice of good Christian friends. Sometimes through prayer. Sometimes by listening to a sermon. Sometimes by an inner conviction that God has spoken to us. Sometimes by a deep sense of inner peace. Sometimes God will guide us through a particular passage of Scripture. Sometimes all of the circumstances of life clearly point in one direction. Sometimes he simply gives us the wisdom to make the right decision. Sometimes he "speaks" to us. Sometimes he guides us by his silence. Very often it is a combination of all of these things put together.

God is committed to guiding his children on their journey from earth to heaven. And though his methods may change, and though sometimes they may be difficult to understand, God is committed to seeing that you ultimately reach your final destination.

Lesson #4:
God's guidance is revealed as we stay close to him

The Old Testament tells us that the cloud and the pillar represented the very presence of God. They weren't just symbols of some heavenly truth; they represented God's presence with his people. We are told in the Old Testament that the Lord spoke from the cloud. So when they saw the cloud, they understood that the Lord himself was leading them.

Do you know what that means? If the cloud went north and you went south, you were soon going to get into trouble. If the cloud started moving and your family didn't follow, you would be separated from the presence of God. And to correct the situation, you would have to turn around and start following the cloud again.

That leads us to a very important conclusion: *God's will is a relationship, not a location.* It is not a question of where you should go or what you should do. Knowing the will of God is not primarily about who you should marry or when you should get married. It's not about taking this job or that job, or how many kids you should have, or where you should go to school, or whether you should be a missionary or not. Those are secondary questions. The primary question is this: *Are you willing to stay close to God and follow wherever he leads you?* It's a spiritual question. When we say to God, "Show me what to do," the Lord says, "Stay close to me." We cry out to the heavens, "I'm scared." God says, "Follow me." We say, "O God, give me some answers." And God says, "Give me your heart."

That's why Numbers 9:23 says, "At the command of the LORD they camped, and at the command of the LORD they set out." If you will do the same thing, God will guide you. If the Lord says stop, you stop. If the Lord says go, you go. He will guide you. The only way to hear God's voice is to stay close to him. This is a moral and spiritual issue. Are you willing to go when he says go, and are you willing to stop when he says stop? If the answer is yes, you can rest assured that God will guide you exactly where he wants you to go. *The secret of knowing God's will is the secret of knowing God; and as you get to know God better, he will reveal his will to you.*

What does that mean for our decision-making? I think it means, when you need to know, you will know. If God is God, and if you are committed to knowing him, staying close to him, and doing his will, then the ultimate responsibility rests on him to make his will clear to you. The issue is not mystical superstition. The issue is, *are you ready to follow God?* If the answer is yes, you may be certain that all your questions about guidance will eventually be answered.

QUESTIONS FOR PERSONAL/GROUP STUDY

1. Sometimes tiny, spur-of-the-moment decisions turn out to have great consequences. Can you think of times in your own experience when what seemed like a small decision at the time came to change your whole life?

2. What is the romance of knowing God's will? List several times in your life when you experienced this romance.

3. How do you feel about the statement, "God wants you to know his will more than you want to know it"? Do you agree with that?

4. If the above statement is true, why do we struggle so often to know God's will?

5. Why does God reveal his will one step at a time instead of all at once? What positive characteristics does the discipline of waiting develop in your life?

6. As you think back to the various turning points of your life, make a list of the different means God has used to reveal his will to you. As you study the list, do you see a pattern in the ways God has guided you?

GOING DEEPER

If you could ask the Lord for specific guidance in any three areas of your life, which areas would you choose? Why? Spend some time in prayer, asking God to give you the guidance you need as you read this book.

2

SENSE AND NONSENSE ABOUT GOD'S WILL

What happened, Lord?" It's a common question, isn't it? You set out to get a new job, you work hard for it, you go through the interview process, you do your very best, and in your heart you believe this is the job God wants you to have. Then someone else gets the job. And you say, "Lord, I thought I was doing your will." Or perhaps you get the job, and you say, "Thank you, Lord." But six months later you're fired, and you say, "What happened, Lord?" Or you think, *If only we could move to Florida, we would be happy.* So you move to Florida, believing it to be the will of God. When you get there, you still are not happy. And you say, "Lord, did we make a mistake?" Deep in our hearts we know God has a plan for us. We don't debate that; it's not a theological issue with us. We *know* that we weren't put on the earth to grope blindly through the darkness. Nevertheless, that's the way life feels sometimes.

Not long ago I listened as my college-age youngest son and one of his friends sat on the couch in our living room talking about this and that. The conversation eventually turned to girls, particularly to one girl who is dating a mutual friend. I listened long enough to discover that they seem to think he should be dating someone else, though the reasons involved seemed obscure to me. After some more discussion, the boys concluded that the relationship would probably end soon anyway. At that point my wife chimed in with the helpful insight that the boy might end it by telling the girl, "I think it's God's will that we break up." She smiled when she said it, and I knew what she was thinking because that's exactly what I said to her when we broke up at the start of our senior year in college. At that time we had been dating for over a year. She had worked at a Christian camp that summer while I took courses at a university several hundred miles away. I hadn't seen her since May but over the summer months had decided we needed to break up. I knew we were falling in love and that marriage was a real possibility if we continued to date, and like most men, that thought terrified me. I was only twenty years old and fairly well convinced that I would probably get married someday, but to me that someday was a few years away.

When I returned to the Christian college we both attended, I decided to do the manly thing and tell her with as much kindness as I could muster that we needed to break up. The scene is etched in my mind. We took a walk one night and ended up in the music building on campus. After a few minutes of awkward conversation (she had no idea what was coming), I told her that I had prayed about it and that I thought it was God's will that we should break up. Though shocked, she took the news gracefully, and we parted on friendly terms. I walked back to my dorm feeling like I had handled a difficult situation pretty well, even though I had some nagging doubts about whether it was really the right thing to do.

Here's the rest of the story. We did not stay broken up very long. After a week or so, I had one of those "light-bulb" moments, and everything suddenly became clear to me. While driving down a country road, I heard a voice say (well, it seemed like I heard a voice—maybe it was just my mind talking to me, trying to get my attention), "Wake up, Ray. You're in love with Marlene." It happened just like that—and it was true. So a few days later I asked to see her again, we got back together, that spring we were engaged, the next August we got married, and we will soon celebrate our thirtieth anniversary.

Looking back I'm not sure how much I meditated on the theological implications of saying it was God's will that we should break up. Since we were both attending a Christian college, it wasn't unusual for a guy (or a girl) to give that reason for ending a relationship. In a sense, it's the ultimate excuse. It's almost like saying, "I'd like to keep dating you, but God won't let me." Who can argue with that? As I think back, I wonder, *Did I really believe it was God's will for us to break up?* But that's putting too much pressure on a nervous college kid who didn't know what to do. Perhaps it truly was God's will for us to break up so that I could realize I had fallen in love with Marlene. Maybe that wouldn't have happened if we hadn't broken up. So maybe I had to say, "It's God will for us to break up" because it was really God's will for us to get back together, get married, and still be together (and happy!) after all these years. As I write these words, it hits me that they express what I truly believe. God's will was done in the end.

That little drama, though hardly earthshaking, illustrates a key truth we often overlook. *Knowing God's will is a journey, not a destination, and along the way we will sometimes be quite confused.* And sometimes we will be flat wrong about what God really wants for us. The bottom line is not being right or wrong about God's will but truly seeking what God's will is in the first place.

OUR SECRET FEAR

The most fundamental question of life is the one that Saul asked on the road to Damascus: "What shall I do, Lord?" (Acts 22:10). In our better moments, we really want to do what the Lord wants us to do. We really do want to stand before the Lord and hear him say, "Well done, good and faithful servant." Many people worry that someday the Lord will say to them, "You did a good job at what you chose to do, but it's not what I sent you to earth to do." Billy Graham said as much to Diane Sawyer in a television interview. When she asked him how it felt to be so successful in evangelism, he replied, "I don't feel that way at all. Most of the time I feel like a failure." That's a shocking statement to hear from a man most people would call the greatest Christian leader of our generation. He went on to say that his greatest goal is to someday hear the Lord Jesus say, "Well done, thou good and faithful servant." Then with some diffidence he added, "But I fear I won't hear him say it."

In the last chapter we discovered that God does indeed desire to guide his children. *If you are willing to follow him, he will lead you exactly where he wants you to go.* There is nothing controversial about that statement. All Christians would agree with it. The problem comes at the next level—the level of practical application. We know God guides his children, but how does that divine guidance work out in the nitty-gritty details? At precisely this point we need to be very clear in our thinking. There is so much misinformation, so much bad teaching, so much faulty theology when we come to the "how-to" of God's guidance. As a result many Christians continually make wrong turns, go down dead-end streets, and end up in spiritual cul-de-sacs because they don't understand what God has said about the way he guides his children.

In order to help us understand the biblical perspective, I'm going to share four wrong ideas about God's guidance and a biblical answer for each one. Each of these myths, though popular, can be devastating to believers.

Myth #1:
God wants you to know the future

This myth is listed first because it is the biggest mistake that Christians make with regard to the will of God. *It is the mistake of assuming the end from the beginning.* Because God has led us one step in a particular direction, we assume that the end result must be guaranteed. We start down a road, and because we are going a certain direction we think the destination is certain. Let's be clear on this one point: *It is rarely God's will for you to know your personal future.* Psalm 119:105 paints a clear picture of how we discover the will of God: "Your word is a lamp to my feet and a light to my path." The picture here is not of a blazing light that illuminates an entire room. It is a picture of a man in total darkness walking along a dangerous trail. There is no moon in the sky. Darkness clings to him. His only light comes from the lantern in his hand. As he holds the lantern, it illuminates the step right in front of him. When he takes that step, what happens to the light? It goes forward one more step. The light is not bright enough to illuminate even ten yards ahead.

Let's face the truth—we want to know the future. At least we think we do. We want to know what is going to happen next year, so we can be ready in advance. But God won't play that game with us.

He Knows—and He's Not Telling

The Bible says, "The secret things belong to the LORD our God" (Deuteronomy 29:29). Does he know what will happen tomorrow? Yes, he does; but he's not telling anyone else about it. Or to put it in familiar terms, does God have a blueprint for your life? Yes, he does; but I don't know any way you can get a copy. My friend Oceile Poage learned she had cancer because of a stomachache that wouldn't go away. After two or three weeks she went to see a doctor, who put her through a battery of tests but couldn't find anything wrong. Months later the diagnosis was finally confirmed—cancer of the stomach lining. Prognosis: slow death. Her chances of survival: 10 percent. One doctor said he had known two patients out of fifty who had survived this particular type of cancer. If she was lucky, she might live four to six months. When the doctors broke the news, they told her, "We can do chemotherapy, but it will make you very sick, and it might not do anything to stop the cancer."

What do you do then? How do you determine God's will? Oceile decided to take chemotherapy as long as she could, but that she would stop if it made her so sick she couldn't enjoy her last days with her family. As is often the case in these situations, Oceile was more at peace about the future than her family was. They didn't want to talk about death. But Oceile wasn't into avoidance. At one point she told me, "I'm not afraid of the future. If I die, I go to be with Jesus. If I live, I get to spend more time with my family and friends. I win either way." Despite the doctor's prediction, Oceile made it to Christmas.

In an apparently unrelated event, on New Year's Eve some friends called us from Los Angeles to say they had found a special airline ticket offer. They could fly from L.A. to Chicago for $140, but they would have to fly back to Los Angeles within twenty-four hours. Would we like to see them? Of course. So they arrived at 9:48 P.M. one night and flew back at 7:00 P.M. the next day. Crazy? Yes, but it's a good crazy, the kind that says, "I have a chance to do this now, and I might not have the chance again."

Right after our friends called from Los Angeles, Marlene and I dropped by Oceile's house to bring her a meal. Christmas had been wonderful for her—not least because she had already lived longer than the doctors expected. She found a book about Michael Jordan that she gave my oldest son as a gift. Two days earlier she had visited a huge antique mall in Indiana with her family. She looked great, except that her hair had fallen out and she had lost lots of weight. Her blood count was down; so they postponed chemotherapy for a few days—a fact that greatly pleased her.

A Final Act of Love

"The doctors don't seem to know whether I'm getting better or not. I wish I knew whether I was living or dying," she said. As everyone who knew her could testify, she was very much alive even though she was dying. Several weeks later she flew to Baltimore with her daughter and husband to visit a ninety-nine-year-old woman who was a longtime friend. Oceile brought food to her friend, cooked a meal, then stayed to talk with her because she wanted to make sure her friend knew Jesus Christ. It was Oceile's final act of love; she died several hours after returning to Chicago. Looking back on her last few weeks, I remembered what her husband said when we told him about our friends flying in from Los Angeles on the spur of the moment. "I think that's the way the Lord wants us to live. Sometimes we wait for our plans to all work out before we do anything. Then it's too late."

I don't know whether he would have said that a year ago. Cancer has a way of bringing you face to face with the fact that no one but God knows what the future holds. As for Oceile, her battle with cancer illustrates the fact that you don't have to know the future in order to know God's will. She died as she had lived— serving others. The cancer simply made each day more precious.

The lesson is clear: *Knowing God's will always involves taking life as it comes, day by day, moment by moment, step by step.*

DOES GOD HAVE A BLUEPRINT OF YOUR LIFE?

That brings us back to the question of the blueprint—the detailed outline of your personal future. Does God have a blueprint that includes everything in your life from the moment of your birth to the moment of your death? Is there a heavenly blueprint that shows what you are supposed to do on October 14, 2012? The answer to that question is, yes. But the only part of it you can see arrives each morning in the form of twenty-four brand-new hours, freshly delivered by United Angel Service Overnight Express. Please don't miss this point: *God wants to teach us to trust him step by step.* He reveals his will one step at a time, so we will trust him moment by moment.

Myth #2:
God wants you to have 100 percent certainty before you make a decision

Many people believe they must be 100 percent certain of God's will before they make a decision. I can understand their thinking. After all, if you are facing a life-changing decision—a potential marriage, a cross-country move, a new career, which college to attend, whether or not to begin chemotherapy—you'd like to know in advance beyond any doubt that you are doing what God wants you to do. There are two problems with this point of view. First, sometimes we think we know God's will with 100 percent certainty only to find out later that we were mistaken. The other problem—which is more common for most believers—is that in our search for certainty about God's will, we end up paralyzed by an inability to make up our minds. Some decisions are so important they can't be left to chance. As the popular saying goes,

"When in doubt, don't." If you aren't sure about the new job, don't take it; don't make the move, don't say yes, don't make any decision with less than total certainty.

But is that good advice? Is it realistic? Is that the way God normally works?

- Did Noah know all about the Flood? No, but he built the ark anyway.
- Did Abraham have a road map? No, but he left Ur of the Chaldees anyway.
- Did Jacob know where he was going or what would happen? No, but he left home because he couldn't safely stay there.
- Did Moses understand what it meant to lead God's people out of Egypt? No, but he said yes when the Lord called him.
- Did Joshua know how the walls were going to come tumbling down? No, but he marched around Jericho anyway.
- Did Gideon fully grasp God's plan to defeat the Midianites? No, he doubted it from the beginning. But God delivered his people anyway.
- Did young David have a clue of what was to come when Samuel said to Jesse, "This is the one"? No, but the Spirit of the Lord came upon him anyway.
- Did Jehoshaphat know how God was going to defeat the Ammonites? No, but he put the singers at the front of the army and sent them out to battle anyway.

We could add a hundred other examples from the Bible. Did the three Hebrew children know how they would be delivered? Was Daniel totally sure the lions would welcome his dropping in on them? Did Peter know he could walk on water? Did Paul know what would happen when he finally got to Rome? The answer is always no. *The life of faith means living with uncertainty even in the midst of doing God's will.* That's the whole point of Hebrews 11. Those great men and women didn't know the future, but they trusted God anyway, sometimes in the face of great personal suffering. And because they kept on believing when circumstances turned against them, they received a great reward.

Too many people want what God has never promised—100 percent certainty before they act. So they wait and wait and they dilly and they dally and they stop and they hesitate and they ruminate. They refuse to go forward because they are waiting for 100 percent certainty. That leads me to this important observation: *It is rarely God's will to give you 100 percent certainty before you make an important decision.*

LOOKING FOR "THE MAN"

We see this principle vividly illustrated in Acts 16. When the apostle Paul and his team left Troas, they sailed across the Aegean Sea in response to a vision of a man saying, "Come over to Macedonia and help us" (v. 9). When they got there, they found a woman named Lydia. But what about "the man"? He was nowhere to be found. Later on Paul and Silas were arrested, stripped, flogged, and thrown in jail. That night during an earthquake they led their jailer to Christ, then baptized him and his whole family. The next morning Paul and Silas were released and escorted out of the city by the town leaders, who were glad to see them go.

It's a strange story. In many ways it appears that Paul failed in Philippi. After all, he was in trouble almost from the moment he arrived. Where was the great church he came to establish? But from God's point of view Paul did exactly what he should have done. He followed God's leading—God gave more light—Paul took another step and waited for further developments. Step by step, through twists and turns and unexpected means, Paul did what God wanted him to do, even though it wasn't what he expected to do when he arrived in town.

TROUBLE IN PARADISE

After sharing these insights with my congregation, I received a letter from a close friend who lives down the street from us. After much planning and prayer and many frustrating delays, she and her husband recently moved into an older house only to discover that it was in much worse shape than they had expected, costing them many thousands of dollars to restore. They also had a long series of unpleasant encounters with a cantankerous neighbor. Looking back on all the difficulties, my friend penned these words:

> Seeking God's will has never caused me much difficulty in the past (partly because I didn't always!), but when we were in the throes of trying to decide about buying this house, we both prayed long and hard that we would have a clear sense of direction and guidance from the Lord or at least a sense of peace about a decision if it were the right one.
>
> Because of the many troubles we've had while living here, I had convinced myself that we made the wrong decision and were paying for it in a big way. Resentment started to taint my relationship with God. Why would He allow us to make such a terrible mistake (expensive one too!) when we spent so much time asking Him for His guidance?
>
> Only in the last few weeks have I felt that God does indeed want us here. Our difficulties in getting here were not God slamming the door shut, but rather Him holding it open just

wide enough for us to squeeze through. Our difficulties in buying the house now seem like good training for the battles while we're in it. Your example from Acts reinforced in my mind this idea and the wrong thinking that was giving me the resentment: that the outcome does not retroactively affect whether it was God's will!

That final sentence is crucial. "The outcome does not retroactively affect whether it was God's will." That's exactly right. *Doing God's will means taking the next step—whatever it is—without a definite promise about the end result.* Many times you won't have 100 percent certainty; but when the moment comes to decide, you must make the best decision you can, trusting God for the results. Sometimes you'll know more, sometimes less; but living by faith means taking the next step anyway.

Myth #3:
God's highest goal is my happiness

Millions of people buy into this false idea. They believe that their happiness is God's supreme goal for them. That sounds good, doesn't it? "God wants me to be happy." "God wants me to be fulfilled." "God wants me to be successful." That thinking has been used to justify all kinds of bizarre and even evil behavior. Some Christian men have said, "It is God's will that I should divorce my wife and marry another woman because we are in love, and God wants us to be happy." The correct theological term for that is, "Baloney."

NOT HAPPY BUT HOLY

If your personal happiness is not God's highest goal for you, then what is God's will for your life? *It is God's will for you to be holy.* It is God's will for you to be like Jesus Christ. It is God's will for you to be in a place of maximum usefulness for the kingdom of God. First Thessalonians 4:3 states this plainly: "This is the will of God, your sanctification" [some translations say, "that you should be holy"]. To be sanctified means to be made holy. It refers to the lifelong process whereby God shapes you, through a myriad of experiences both positive and negative, into the image of Jesus Christ. Here's the clincher: *He uses the very worst things that happen to us in order to accomplish his divine purposes in us.*

"She's Still My Wife"

A close friend of mine found himself put to the test when, after many happy years of marriage, his wife suddenly developed Alzheimer's disease. Her descent from rationality happened so fast that even the doctors were surprised. At first my friend hired a housekeeper to take care of his wife, but that solution did not work for long. Soon he admitted her to a nursing home with a special unit for patients with Alzheimer's.

The first time he took me to visit her, I was not prepared for what I saw. The woman I had known—vibrant and full of life—had simply disappeared. In her place was a feeble old woman barely able to feed herself. But when we walked in, she recognized her husband and called him by name. We walked arm-in-arm down the hall together, listening to her chatter away aimlessly, her words and sentences tumbling out unconnected as if some inner computer had been tampered with and the wires hopelessly crossed. Toward the end of our visit, when her husband asked if she would like me to pray for her, she said, "Yes, that would be nice," then stared blankly into space while I prayed. As we left to go home, we got into separate cars. My friend brushed the tears from his eyes before he drove away.

But that is only part of the story. My friend also has a very successful career that takes him around the world. More than that, his work repeatedly puts him in business meetings at some of the most glamorous resort areas known to man. He is strong, has a charismatic personality, is visibly successful, and is one of the most respected men in his field. By the world's standards, he has it all. I asked him at one point why he remained faithful to his marriage vows. There was no chance—none whatsoever—that his wife would get better.

"I Made a Promise"

My friend answered, "Simple. I made a promise, and I have to keep it. Years ago when I pledged to be faithful to my wife, I didn't know she would have Alzheimer's disease. But she made the same promise to me. It could have happened to me instead of her. As a Christian, I simply have no choice but to be faithful no matter what happens." Lest that sound grim and hopeless, he added these words: "Since my wife has developed Alzheimer's disease, I have gone through the hardest time of my life. Yet out of that hard time, God has drawn me closer to himself than I've ever been before. If I were unfaithful, I would lose all I have gained in my walk with the Lord. I would be a double loser then. My wife is contributing all she can to the marriage. The fact that she's locked up for her own safety doesn't change that fact. Even though she barely recognizes me now, we're still married. I've made a promise to her, and I'm going to keep it."

"My Son Has Been Watching You"

Before she died, his wife regressed to the point that she no longer could communicate with anyone. In the end she sat motionless in a chair, her hands clenched, her legs permanently crossed. The doctors have no idea what kept her alive so long except that somewhere deep inside her a spark of life kept burning. One day her husband said to me, "I don't know why she is still alive. I can't see any purpose in it. Why is God allowing her to hang on when the person I knew disappeared years ago?" My friend wasn't complaining but was just stating the facts as he saw them. He was still faithful, but the road was hard, the nights long, the loneliness intense, the future bleak.

Then my friend spent an evening with a man who told him, "You'll never know what you have meant to my son. He's been watching you take care of your wife all these years. You don't know it, but he's been talking about you to everyone he meets. He tells them that anyone else would have left her by now and started a new life. But you didn't do that. You stayed with her. And that has made a profound impression on my son." My friend told me, "Maybe that's it. Maybe God allowed this so that somehow through it all I could help someone else." Nothing I have said can lessen the terrible pain my friend endured. But he would tell you that God has changed his life profoundly through the experience of watching his wife die. He would also say that God has seen fit to use this to reach many people for Jesus Christ.

Is my friend happy? That depends on the circumstances of any given day. But there is unmistakable joy in spite of everything and a hard-won faith in the goodness of God.

With that, we come to the final myth.

Myth #4:
God makes his will hard to find

Many people struggle unnecessarily in this area. Perhaps they are seeking 100 percent certainty, or maybe they are seeking some kind of message from God—a postcard that reads, "Dear Jack, Buy the red Pontiac. Signed, God." Or they fear that one night, while they are watching *Monday Night Football*, God will reveal his will, and they will somehow miss it. Or they worry that they have sinned too much and have blown their only chance to do God's will.

"TRUST ME"

To all these things God says, "Trust me." *God wants you to know his will more than you want to know it.* God is more committed to showing you his will than you are to discovering it. He takes full responsibility for getting you from here to there step by step. He has said, "I will never leave you" (Hebrews 13:5). And he won't. He also said, "I will instruct you and teach you in the way you should go" (Psalm 32:8). And he will. He also promised, "I am with you always" (Matthew 28:20). And he is.

We think that God's will is hard to find. The biblical perspective is quite different. *God will reveal his will to anyone who is willing to do it.* That leads me to one final thought: *God ordinarily will not show you his will in order for you to consider it.* He won't show you his will so you can say, "Maybe I will . . . maybe I won't. How about Plan B, Lord?" He will show you his will when he knows you are willing to do it.

John 7:17 makes this truth very plain. Jesus said to the Jews, "If anyone's will is to do God's will, he will know whether the teaching is from God or whether I am speaking on my own authority." Concentrate on that first phrase—"If anyone's will is to do God's will." You have to choose before you know. If you want to know God's will, you have to choose to do it before you know what it is. You don't say, "Lord, show me, and then I'll decide what I am going to do." The Lord says, "No, you decide to obey me, and then I will show you what I want you to do." Let me boil it down to one rather astounding statement: *If you are willing to do God's will, you will do it.* The only thing that is required is a total willingness on your part to do God's will, and you will do it. Step by step. Moment by moment. Day by day. If you are willing to do God's will, you will do it because he will see to it.

Is that easy? Yes and no. It's not easy because everything in this world pulls you away from God. But it is easy in the sense that you can truly do God's will if you want to.

That leaves us with two penetrating questions. First, *do you want to know God's will?* If the answer is no or if you are not sure, then let me ask the second question: *Are you willing to be made willing?* Maybe that's where we need to end this chapter. Are you willing to be made willing? If you will say, "Lord, I am not sure I am willing, but I am willing to be made willing," he will lead you step by step. If you are willing to do his will, you will do it.

QUESTIONS FOR PERSONAL/GROUP STUDY

1. Why is it important that you ask God for guidance? What happens when you skip this important first step?
2. Can you think of a time when you thought you understood God's will only to find out later that things didn't work out exactly as you expected? Why does God let that happen to us?
3. How do you feel about the statement, "It is rarely God's will for you to know your personal future"? Does that discourage you in any way? Suppose you had known in advance everything that was going to happen to you in the last ten years. How would that knowledge have changed your life? Suppose God offered to show you the next ten years in detail. Would you take him up on that offer? Why or why not?
4. Think of a time when a seemingly trivial event turned out to change the course of your life. What does that teach you about the way God's will unfolds in your life?
5. How do you feel about the statement, "If you are willing to do God's will, you will do it"?

6. What is the number one factor keeping you from doing God's will right now? Is there something holding you back? What is it?

GOING DEEPER

Make a list of the five biggest decisions you've made in your life. Next to each decision, write yes or no to this question: At the time, did you believe you were doing God's will? Then write a sentence or two giving your long-range evaluation of how that decision turned out. What conclusions do you draw about the way God works in your life?

3

Don't Get Fleeced!

Beginning with this chapter, we are taking a sharp right turn in our quest to discover God's will. Up till now we've surveyed various biblical passages in order to draw out some basic principles. Now we are going to look at some of the common problems and questions associated with the will of God. The first question concerns putting out a fleece. You may have heard of this somewhere along the way even if you don't know what it means. Putting out a fleece or fleecing (whether or not the term is understood or used) is a common technique for determining God's will.

What Is a Fleece?

In its most general sense, *putting out a fleece refers to seeking to learn the will of God by means of a predetermined sign*. People generally use a fleece when they come to a point of decision and don't know what to do. Maybe you're faced with a job offer and don't know whether to say yes or no. So you say to God, "Please give me a sign." For instance, "If they offer me a salary that is twenty thousand dollars more than my current salary, I'll take that as a sign from God that I should accept the job." In that case, the twenty thousand dollars would be the fleece. You are putting out a fleece when you say, "God, I am asking you to give me a sign, and this is the sign I want you to give me." It's that second part that really qualifies as putting out a fleece. It's not just asking for guidance. It's when you say, "Lord, I want you to do such-and-such, and if you will do what I have asked, I will know what your will is."

WHAT IS THE BIBLICAL BACKGROUND FOR FLEECING?

In order to answer this question, let's travel back in time some thirty-three hundred years to meet a man named Gideon. The angel of the Lord came to him one day and said, "The LORD is with you, O mighty man of valor" (Judges 6:12). This surprising word came in the midst of the Midianite oppression of Israel. The Midianites were a vast army from the east who invaded Israel riding on camels. They came each year during harvesttime just as the Israelites were reaping their crops. They would plunder the land, get on their camels, ride out of town, and then stay away until the next year's harvest. Then they would come back and do it all over again. So every year at harvesttime the Jews were losing everything they had worked for because of the Midianites' invasion. The people of God were reduced to living in caves because they were frightened of the mighty power of the Midianites.

In response to this crisis God tapped Gideon on the shoulder and said, "I am going to use you to deliver my people." The angel of the Lord (probably a pre-incarnate appearance of Jesus Christ) was very clear on that point. "Gideon, you're the man who will deliver my people." He repeated it two or three times in Judges 6. Gideon responded, "Who . . . me?" "Yes, you." "You've got the wrong man." "No, I don't. You're the man, Gideon."

The following verses detail the various things God did to convince Gideon that he was indeed the right man for the job. First, *Gideon asked for a sign from God so he would know that he was really talking to the angel of the Lord* (v. 17). When Gideon placed his offering on a rock, the angel touched the meat and the bread with the tip of his staff. "Fire sprang up from the rock and consumed the flesh and the unleavened cakes" (v. 21). Gideon correctly concluded from this supernatural sign that the angelic visitor was genuine. He says as much in verse 22: "Alas, O Lord GOD! For now I have seen the angel of the LORD face to face." When God assured him he was not going to die, Gideon built an altar to commemorate the event.

Second, *God directed Gideon to tear down his father's altar to Baal and to build an altar to the Lord.* When Gideon tore down the pagan altar, he and his men did so at night because they were afraid of public reaction (v. 27). As it turned out, his fear was well-founded because the people of Ophrah were ready to put him to death the next morning. But his father intervened, reasoning that Baal could defend himself and didn't need any help from the townspeople.

Third, when the Midianites prepared for their annual invasion, *the Spirit of the Lord came upon Gideon in great power, equipping him to lead the people of God* (v. 34). He sent messengers to Manasseh and the neighboring tribes, calling the men to battle.

All was now set for the showdown between the men of Israel and the invading Midianites. God had found his leader—the reluctant Gideon—and had reaffirmed his call through a miraculous sign, had protected him from a lynch mob, and had filled him with the Holy Spirit. The men were gathered, the enemy was approaching, and everyone was ready for the great battle. Everyone, that is, except Gideon. He was still not sure if he was the right man to lead Israel.

GIDEON KNEW!

Before we look at the story of the fleece, note this fact: *Judges 6 is perfectly clear that Gideon knew exactly what God wanted him to do.* The fleece was simply meant to *confirm* God's will, not to *determine* God's will. He actually said as much in Judges 6:36— "If you will save Israel by my hand, *as you have said.*" Verse 37 says, "Then I shall know that you will save Israel by my hand, *as you have said*" (italics added). No matter what conclusion you come to about the modern practice of fleecing, remember that originally it was used to *confirm* God's will, not to *determine* it.

Gideon is one of the most fearful men in all the Bible. Although he was a great hero, he was also filled with fear. In contemporary terms, he was a man with low self-esteem. He didn't feel very good about himself. Gideon doubted that God could use him to deliver Israel. So in spite of everything else that had happened, he asked God to give him one more confirming sign. Judges 6:36-40 sets the scene for us:

> Then Gideon said to God, "If you will save Israel by my hand, as you have said, behold, I am laying a fleece of wool on the threshing floor. If there is dew on the fleece alone, and it is dry on all the ground, then I shall know that you will save Israel by my hand, as you have said." And it was so. When he rose early next morning and squeezed the fleece, he wrung enough dew from the fleece to fill a bowl with water. Then Gideon said to God, "Let not your anger burn against me; let me speak just once more. Please let me test just once more with the fleece. Please let it be dry on the fleece only, and on all the ground let there be dew." And God did so that night; and it was dry on the fleece only, and on all the ground there was dew.

The first time the sheepskin was soaking wet, so much so that Gideon squeezed out a bowlful of water. That makes sense because a sheepskin would draw the moisture out of the air. The only unusual fact was that the ground was bone-dry. That was unusual, but it was not absolutely *impossible*. Gideon was still not sure; so he timidly asked God to do it again, only backwards—the ground wet and the sheepskin dry. That would be much more unusual because the fleece would normally get wet from the dew. The next morning the ground was wet, and the fleece was bone-dry. The message is clear. Gideon received double confirmation of what he already knew to be the will of God. Judges 7 goes on to tell the amazing story of how God used Gideon in a very unlikely way to win a great battle with the Midianites.

NOT THE SAME

Before we move on, let's nail down the central point. *The way most people today use fleecing is not the same way Gideon did.* We use the fleece today when we are uncertain about what God wants us to do. We don't know if we should get married or not; we're not sure if we should send our kids to a public school or a Christian school; we're torn between two good job offers; we don't know whether to move to the suburbs or stay in the city. We use a fleece when we don't know the will of God. But Gideon already knew God's will. That's a crucial issue. The fleece was never used to *determine* God's will. The only time that it was ever used was to *confirm* God's will, which had already been made unmistakably clear.

Typically people today use fleecing as a predetermined sign to ascertain God's will. "I'm thinking about buying a new car. I don't know whether I should or not. Lord, if you will send me five hundred dollars by tomorrow afternoon, I'll know it's your will for me to buy a new car." Or maybe your boss offers you a new job. Should you take it or not? So you say, "Lord, if my boss calls me between 2:00 and 3:00 this afternoon, I will know it is your will for me to take this job." Perhaps you are thinking about moving to another city. You have a decision to make. Should you move or not? So you say, "Lord, I'm not sure what you want me to do, but if I wake up tomorrow morning and there are four inches of snow on the ground, I will know it is your will for me to move."

Let's suppose you are in college and find yourself becoming interested in a young man you see three times a week in your Advanced Ceramic Design class. You are wondering if this is the guy for you. So you say, "Lord, when I see him after class tomorrow, if he smiles at me, that will be a sign that we should get married." That's a fleece. It's a predetermined sign that you use in order to determine God's will. Christians use fleeces all the time when facing major life decisions.

All of which brings us to the second important question.

What Kind of Faith Did Gideon Have?

Gideon was a man of very weak faith. Hebrews 11:32 makes it clear that he did have faith. But the record in Judges 6 shows that his faith—though genuine—was weak. In Judges 6:12 the angel of the Lord appears to Gideon and says, "The LORD is with you, O mighty man of valor." Gideon immediately starts to argue. He sees all the problems and none of the possibilities. "How can I be a mighty warrior? Where is God? Where are all the miracles?"

The angel of the Lord answers, "Go in this might of yours and save Israel from the hand of Midian; do not I send you?" (v. 14). Immediately Gideon starts to argue again: "Please, Lord, how can I save Israel? Behold, my clan is the weakest in Manasseh, and I am the least in my father's house" (v. 15). The Lord answers, "I will be with you, and you shall strike the Midianites as one man" (v. 16).

"Not me. You've got the wrong guy, Lord. I think you've

made a mistake. I come from Manasseh. Nobody great comes from Manasseh. And my family is the weakest of all the families in Manasseh. And I'm the least in my own family."

So Gideon asks the angel to let him bring an offering as a sign that God is going to use him. The offering is immediately consumed with fire (vv. 17-21). It's an absolute miracle. So Gideon gets the sign he asks for.

We must evaluate the fleece episode against that background. Three times the angel said, "You are the man." Then Gideon asked for and received a miraculous sign that he was the one. After all that, he was *still* unsure. "Lord, I know what you want me to do, but I still have my doubts. I'm insecure. I feel inferior. I don't feel up to the task." When the fleece is wet and the ground is dry, even *that* is not enough. You can hear his apology in the words he uses—"Let not your anger burn against me; let me speak just once more" (v. 39).

Let me state one fact very clearly. I am not suggesting that what Gideon did was wrong. It was not a sin to ask God for a fleece; but it was a sign of his weak faith because he already knew what God wanted him to do. If you make that a habit or a pattern in your life, it is a sign of weak faith in your life. When you look at Gideon's life, you don't see a man of great robust faith— you see a man of weak faith whom God nevertheless used greatly.

What Does the New Testament Say About Fleecing?

The answer is, nothing at all. However, that's a significant point. *There are no examples in the New Testament where anyone ever put out a fleece in order to determine God's will—or even to confirm it.* And you only find it once in the Old Testament. You never read any passage where the apostle Paul advises the believers at

Rome or Philippi or Ephesus to put out a fleece to determine God's will. There are no examples of anything like that in the New Testament.

CASTING LOTS

Some people have found a parallel in the story of the eleven apostles casting lots in Acts 1 to find a replacement for Judas. They nominated two men—Joseph and Matthias. They then cast lots, and the lot fell to Matthias; so he was added to the eleven apostles. First of all, this is not parallel to Judges 6 because the apostles truly didn't know which man God had chosen. Second, casting lots was an Old Testament practice that is used in Acts 1 as a kind of holdover during the transitional period before Pentecost and the birth of the church through the descent of the Holy Spirit. Third, casting lots was a recognized and oft-repeated Old Testament practice, but putting out a fleece happened only once and was never repeated. In light of all that, it's hard to see how Acts 1 parallels Judges 6 in any meaningful way.

LOOKING FOR A SIGN

In Matthew 12:38-39 the Pharisees asked Jesus for a miraculous sign to prove he was the promised Messiah. "An evil and adulterous generation seeks for a sign," Jesus replied. Please meditate on that carefully. *Demanding miraculous signs from God is not necessarily a sign of strong faith*. It is often a sign of a very weak and immature faith. In this case it was a cover for an unbelieving heart. Jesus repeats his words in Matthew 16:1-4. When the Jewish leaders came asking for a sign from heaven, Jesus said, "An evil and adulterous generation seeks for a sign, but no sign will be given to it except the sign of Jonah." The sign of the prophet Jonah was a reference to Christ's coming resurrection from the dead. He was saying, "I've already told you everything you need to know about what God can do. Why do you come asking me for something extra?"

DOUBTING THOMAS

Then we have the case of Thomas—the man who would not believe in the resurrection of Christ until he put his hands into the wounded side of Jesus. Jesus didn't humiliate him or belittle his lack of faith. "Then he said to Thomas, 'Put your finger here, and see my hands; and put out your hand, and place it in my side. Do not disbelieve, but believe'" (John 20:27). Jesus met him at the point of his weakness. But what did Jesus say next? "Have you believed because you have seen me? Blessed are those who have not seen and yet have believed" (20:29). There is one level of the Christian life that says, "Lord, you have to show me first. I have to see a sign before I will believe." There is another level that says, "Lord, you said it. I don't see any signs, but I believe what you said." It's better to say, "Lord, I'm going to do your will signs or no signs, fleece or no fleece."

When you know God's will, you are to do it. Period. End of discussion. It is a weak form of Christianity that says to the Almighty, "You must meet my conditions before I will do your will." Second Corinthians 5:7 offers the biblical perspective: "We live by faith, not by sight." You can say this another way: We live by faith, not by fleeces.

WHAT ARE THE DANGERS OF FLEECING?

I'll mention three answers to that question. First, *fleecing often leads to uncertainty and confusion*. What about the man who says, "I'll buy this car if the Lord sends me five hundred dollars tomorrow"? What do you do if the next day you get 485 dollars? Do you say, "Close enough"? No. You asked God for five hundred dollars. Does it have to be *exactly* five hundred dollars, or are we talking ballpark numbers here? There's no way to answer a question like that with any certainty. Since you made up the "rules," is it okay to bend them, or are you then guilty of trying to help God out?

The second danger is that *fleecing comes very close to attempting to manipulate God.* The Bible repeatedly warns us against putting God to the test. What does it mean to put God to the test? *It is any attempt to box him in according to our human understanding.* "Lord, if you are going to work, let me tell you exactly how you have to work in my life." Let's go back to the example of the person who says, "I'll take the new job if my boss calls me between 2:00 and 3:00 P.M." Fine, but what if your boss calls at 1:30 P.M.? You have boxed God into a sixty-minute period in your life. And that's a way of putting God to the test.

The third problem is this: *You end up shifting responsibility from yourself to God, thus destroying the need for faith.* That brings us again to a fundamental insight regarding God's will. Generally speaking it is not God's plan to show you your personal future. More often, God shows you the next step and that's all. Too many times fleecing is an attempt to force God to show you the future. When I shared this with my congregation, someone said, "Your sermon on fleecing made one thing very clear. You still have to choose." He's right. You still have to take responsibility for your choices. Fleecing is an attempt to shift responsibility for our decisions from us to God, thus destroying the need for faith and responsible decision-making. Too often we want to know the future when God's will is merely to show us the next step we should take.

But you still have to choose. After all the prayer, all the Bible study, all the counsel, all the meditation, all the writing down of options, after you've agonized, still the moment comes when you must decide. God won't take the responsibility for you. If you're going to take that new job, you have to decide for yourself. If you are going to sell your house, you can't wait for God to write a message in the clouds. You have to sign the papers yourself. God isn't going to do it for you. Fleecing is an attempt to stand at the fork in the road forever without making a decision. It destroys the need for faith and decisive action. But to put the matter that way leaves out an important perspective.

IS IT ALWAYS WRONG TO ASK FOR A SIGN?

The answer is no. It's not wrong to ask for a sign if you are simply asking for guidance as to the next step you should take. "Father, make your will plain so I will know the next step." Is that a fleece? No, because you are not boxing God in. You are just asking God to do what he said he would do—to make plain the path you should follow. But it is boxing God in if you say, "Lord, in order to know the next step, I want my boss to call between 2:00 and 3:00 in the afternoon." That comes close to black magic and superstition. There's a huge difference between asking for guidance and trying to squeeze God into a mold of your own making. We should say, "Lord, I stand on the verge of making a big decision. I need to know the next step I should take. I pray that you will make it clear to me."

Sometimes asking for a sign is nothing more than using sanctified common sense. In Matthew 10:11-16 Jesus advises his disciples on how to discern God's will in certain situations:

> *Whatever town or village you enter, find out who is worthy in it and stay there until you depart. As you enter the house, greet it. And if the house is worthy, let your peace come upon it, but if it is not worthy, let your peace return to you. And if anyone will not receive you or listen to your words, shake off the dust from your feet when you leave that house or town. Truly, I say to you, it will be more bearable on the day of judgment for the*

land of Sodom and Gomorrah than for that town. Behold, I am sending you out as sheep in the midst of wolves, so be wise as serpents and innocent as doves.

Jesus instructs his followers to look for certain outward indicators in order to find God's will. He gives them a very simple strategy: "If they listen, stay there; if not, go someplace else. Shake the dust off your feet." That's not a fleece. It's using common sense to properly analyze the situation and to draw good conclusions regarding what God wants you to do. That's what I mean by sanctified common sense.

Is it always wrong to ask for a sign? No; not if you are simply asking for guidance and not trying to box God in.

What Is the Essential Difference Between a Sign and a Fleece?

With this question we come directly to the heart of the issue. One essential difference is that a fleece is an unusual event unrelated to the particular guidance you need. For instance, finding snow on the ground does not necessarily signal that you should move to Florida. Likewise, seeing clouds shaped like penguins doesn't mean God is calling you to be a missionary to Antarctica. This isn't to say that God couldn't arrange the circumstances of life to cause these things to happen or that he might not use them in your life. But there is no *necessary* connection between the unusual event and the guidance desired.

That brings us back to Judges 6 and Gideon's fleece. The sign was *clear*, it was *unmistakable*, and it was *miraculous*. So what's wrong with that? Nothing, really. Gideon asked for an unrelated sign, and God granted his request. However, the request came from weak faith, and the requested sign had nothing to do with whether or not the Midianites would be defeated. Presumably

Gideon could have asked for some other sign, which God could have given him.

For the reasons I've already mentioned, I don't recommend the practice of asking for unrelated, specific signs as a means of determining God's will. It is fraught with too many difficulties and possible misinterpretations.

"THE DEVIL COULD HAVE SENT US $23,500"

However, there are times when asking for a *related* sign may be the course of wisdom. Early in his ministry Billy Graham was considering an offer to begin a nationwide radio ministry. It seemed like a good idea, but where would the funds come from to support such a venture? It would be far worse to start a radio ministry only to see it fail than never to start at all. It happened that the offer came during a crusade in Portland, Oregon. After praying about it, Billy decided to ask God for a sign to indicate if he should go ahead with the idea. Specifically, he asked God to bring in twenty-five thousand dollars by midnight of that same day if God wanted the radio ministry to begin. It's crucial to note at this point that twenty-five thousand dollars was more than just a sign; it represented the initial start-up costs for the ministry. It's also important to know that Graham felt that the radio ministry should be supported by many people—not just by a few rich contributors. That's why he decided to ask the crusade audience to support this new idea *that very day*. Thus, the sign requested—and even the timing of it—was directly related to the guidance desired.

After the service that night, people lined up to give money to the new project. When everything was counted, the total came to 23,500 dollars. The two men proposing the radio ministry suggested that was close enough. "The devil could give us 23,500 dollars," Billy replied. It had to be at least twenty-five thousand dollars. The team returned to their hotel feeling somewhat dejected. Shortly before midnight, one of Billy's coworkers went to the hotel desk where he was given three envelopes. When he opened them, he found they contained cash and pledges for exactly fifteen hundred dollars. The "fleece" had been met exactly as Billy Graham had prayed it would a few hours earlier.

My only comment—other than to marvel at God's miraculous provision—is that this isn't exactly parallel to what Gideon did. Gideon knew God's will; Billy Graham didn't. Gideon's sign was unrelated to the guidance needed. The twenty-five thousand dollars was directly related to the expenses necessary to start the *Hour of Decision* radio program. And asking the crusade audience to support this new project *that night* demonstrated the wide support necessary to make the radio ministry successful over the long haul.

Don't miss the larger point here: Asking for a sign isn't wrong, especially when the sign is directly related to the guidance you need. But simply asking for a sign from God isn't necessarily putting out a fleece. It may simply be using sanctified common sense in a given situation. "If the money comes in, we'll start. If not, we won't." I can see nothing wrong with that approach to determining God's will if it is used in conjunction with other indicators such as prayer, searching the Scriptures, and listening to wise counsel.

Let's wrap up this chapter with three concise conclusions regarding fleecing.

Conclusion #1:
Fleecing can be dangerous, misleading, and manipulative and can lead to a subjective faith in God

That statement should make my position clear. I've already said that many believers use this method to determine God's will. I've done it myself. *If this is your habitual pattern for finding God's will, stop.* This is not the best way because you are in danger of trying to put God in a box. If you haven't used this method of finding God's will, don't start, because it can easily lead you to make a foolish decision.

Conclusion #2:
Seeking wisdom and putting out a fleece are different

Seeking wisdom simply means asking God for his direction for the next step without boxing him in. Putting out a fleece is an attempt to limit God in order to discover the future. And that's not valid. God will show you the next step, but he is not committed to showing you the future.

It also helps to remember that seeking wisdom involves looking at relevant circumstances. Saying, "I won't buy that car unless I have three thousand dollars in the bank" is not asking for a fleece; it's simply a prudent financial decision. But saying, "If it snows on July 4th, I'll know God wants me to move to Detroit" is foolish because you are asking for a sign that has no relation to the decision you are making. A fleece involves selecting an arbitrary or unrelated sign that actually attempts to force God's hand by causing him to reveal the future. Wisdom means asking God for specific guidance involving the relevant circumstances of the decision you need to make. You may need to think about that for a bit, but the distinction is both real and crucial.

Conclusion #3:
Mature faith relies less on spectacular signs and more on wisdom from God and sanctified common sense

That sentence sums up this entire chapter. Is it wrong to put out a fleece? No, it's not wrong. Is it unwise? In my opinion, the answer is yes. Does God guide his children? Yes, he does. Does that mean we have to put out a fleece in order to help him do it? The answer to that is no. Our problem is, we want to stay at the baby level of Christianity. We want to stay in spiritual diapers so we won't have to take responsibility for our own decisions. That's why we constantly ask for signs, though what we need to do is trust God and then take decisive action.

What is it that God wants from us? Simple faith. No one has ever improved on the words of Solomon: "Trust in the LORD with all your heart, and do not lean on your own understanding. In all your ways acknowledge him, and he will make straight your paths" (Proverbs 3:5-6). "In all your ways," not "in all your fleeces." There is a difference.

Our Father wants to bring us to the place where our trust is in him alone, not in circumstances or in fleeces. He wants to bring us to the point where we are willing to move out at his command with signs or without them. There's a phrase for this: *naked faith*. God wants us to have faith in him apart from the circumstances, apart from the fleeces, apart from our own scheming and manipulation—nothing but faith in him alone. *Trust in the Lord with all your heart, and—with or without fleeces—he will direct your paths.*

QUESTIONS FOR PERSONAL/GROUP STUDY

1. Probably the most difficult aspect of this chapter is properly defining fleecing as it relates to the will of God. Take a few moments to read Judges 6 carefully. How much did Gideon know about God's will before putting out the fleece? Why did he ask for this additional sign?

2. Gideon was a man of weak faith. As you read Judges 6, at what points did he demonstrate faith, and at what points did his doubt come through?

3. How would you have responded if you had been in Gideon's situation?

4. Can you think of any times when you were facing a tough decision and you put out a fleece? What happened? What lessons did you learn from those experiences? Under what circumstances, if any, would you advise a friend to put out a fleece?

5. According to this chapter, the crucial element in putting out a fleece is asking for an unrelated sign. List the dangers of this practice.

6. What is the fundamental difference between asking for guidance and putting out a fleece?

GOING DEEPER

Tony just graduated from high school and is trying to decide where to go to college. He has narrowed his choices down to a local community college, a Christian college in another state, and a large university about seventy-five miles from home. After praying about it, he decided to apply to all three colleges, believing that he should attend the first college that accepted him. Letters of acceptance from all three schools arrive on the very same day. Confused, he comes to you for help. How would you advise him to proceed?

4

DREAMS, VISIONS, AND SUPERNATURAL SIGNS

I know a Christian man who fell deeply in love with a young lady he met when she came to his country on a short-term missions trip. After a few days together, he truly thought that God wanted them to get married. When she returned to America, he wrote her saying that he knew it was God's will because one day he looked up in the sky and saw a white bird and a black bird flying together. In the same letter he also said that while walking by a stream, he saw two fish swimming together. As he watched, they seemed to kiss each other. What greater evidence could he ask for? Surely this was a sign from God!

Whenever dreams, visions, and supernatural signs are discussed, three questions immediately come to mind. Number 1: Are such things really possible today? Number 2: If they are, what part do they have in determining God's will for your life? Number 3: If you think you have had a dream, vision, or some kind of supernatural experience, what guidelines should you follow in evaluating that experience?

It's certainly easy to go to extremes in this whole area. Some people argue that dreams, visions, and supernatural signs from God simply cannot and will not happen today. If you move to the other end of the spectrum, others believe that such things should be a normal and regular part of the Christian life. And between those two views you can find evangelicals at virtually every possible point along the spectrum, from "It might happen, but I doubt it" to "It could happen occasionally" to "God often communicates this way" to "You should expect signs and wonders in your life" to "You should seek supernatural signs" to "Signs and wonders are for all Christians all the time." With this in mind, I want to suggest that the truth lies somewhere between the extremes of never and always.

WISHING FOR A MIRACLE

One point I have stressed in this book is that *discovering God's will is a step-by-step process.* Trying to discover what God wants you to do is not something you do early in the morning while you are getting dressed. It's a process. After all, most of life's decisions are very difficult. Some of them are extremely complex. Often we come to the moment of decision and truly don't know what to do. It is at those moments that we wish God would speak directly to us. We dream of going upstairs in the morning to the second-floor window, looking outside, and finding a message from God written in four-foot-tall letters in the grass below: "Go to China and be a missionary." "Sell your house and move to Vermont." "Enroll in medical school." "Don't worry about your grandmother. She's going to be fine." "Don't marry Frank. Marry Ed instead."

Some Christians claim to have experiences of that nature on a fairly regular basis. They leave the impression that whenever they come to a point of decision, God somehow miraculously speaks to them. The problem is, for every person who fits into that category there are many others who go for years and even for a lifetime and never have anything mystical or seemingly supernatural happen at all. It is possible for those who find themselves in that second category to begin to feel like second-class citizens. If you listen to the people in that first group very long, you may begin to wonder, *Is something wrong with me? Am I not praying enough? Am I not godly enough?*

I regard myself as being in this second category. Although there have been a few occasions when it seemed that God was speaking supernaturally to me, those moments have been few and far between. My conclusions in this chapter come in part from my personal experience and in part from many conversations with Christians who are confused about dreams, visions, and supernatural signs. The biblical material comes from several years of study and theological reflection, from which I have discerned five basic truths.

Truth #1:
In Bible times God often revealed his will through supernatural means

The key word is "often." There are many examples of God speaking supernaturally at certain points in biblical history. For instance, the Bible records God's conversation with Adam and Eve, his instructions to Noah to build an ark, his call to Abraham in Ur of the Chaldees, the story of Moses and the burning bush, Jacob's ladder, Joseph's dream, Gideon's fleece, Samuel hearing the voice of the Lord, Daniel's vision of the four creatures, the handwriting on the wall, Joseph being warned in a dream to take the baby Jesus to Egypt, Peter's vision of the animals being lowered out of heaven, Paul's encounter with Jesus on the Damascus Road, and Paul's vision of the man from Macedonia. In this category we ought also to put John's vision on the Isle of Patmos, which makes up most of the book of Revelation. Even a casual reading of the Bible confirms that God often communicated using supernatural means.

Truth #2:
God did not communicate this way all the time, nor did he do it for all the people in the Bible

Some commentators have observed that many of the supernatural events occurred during three crucial time periods: Moses and the exodus from Egypt, the days of Elijah and Elisha, and the life of Christ and the first few years of the Christian church. To make that observation is not to deny that God revealed himself supernaturally to the patriarchs and through the prophets of Israel. But clearly there were periods of time in the Old Testament when no unusual, miraculous manifestations took place. Abraham evidently didn't hear directly from God every day; neither did Jacob or Elijah or Daniel. As far as we know, the average Israelite in Beersheba or the average Christian living in Cappadocia may have lived his entire life without ever experiencing any supernatural revelation from God.

Truth #3:
God spoke supernaturally at critical moments of history

He spoke to Abraham when he called him to leave Ur of the Chaldees. He spoke to Joseph when he wanted to reveal his plan for the nation of Israel. He spoke to Moses when he called him to lead his people out of Egypt. In Acts 10 he gave Peter the vision of the clean and unclean animals being lowered together out of heaven when he wanted Peter to understand that the Gospel was not just for the Jews but also for the Gentiles. In Acts 16 he spoke to Paul supernaturally when he wanted Paul to understand that he wasn't to stay in Asia Minor but was to move west into Greece and eventually on to Rome.

If you begin to look at these events, one pattern emerges: *God used supernatural means to communicate his will at critical moments of history.* Abraham had to leave Ur so God could raise up the nation of Israel. Moses needed to lead the children of Israel from Egypt to Canaan. Peter had to learn that the Gospel is not for Jews only, but for Gentiles as well. Paul had to discover that God had chosen him to take the Gospel to Europe.

This point, if not pressed too far, may be useful in helping us think about various supernatural signs that may happen today. I can find no particular biblical objection to the notion that at some critical juncture in your life God *might* (here I speak with due caution) use some unusual event to confirm his will to you. Such things did happen occasionally in the Bible, though not every day and not to every person. Therefore, it doesn't seem wise to rule them out completely today.

Truth #4:
There are some dangers associated with focusing on dreams and visions and the supernatural

There are at least three dangers in focusing on supernatural events in your Christian life. First, there is the danger of elevating the unusual over the ordinary. Second, there is the danger of elevating your personal experience over the Word of God. Third, there is a very real possibility that you will actually miss God's guidance because you are focusing on the spectacular and on the unusual when God might be revealing his plan for you through the ordinary circumstances of life.

Truth #5:
God may use supernatural means to lead his people today

We know that he did so in biblical times. We also know that his power is the same today as then. However, that does not prove that at any given moment God will speak supernaturally today. I'm not sure how one would prove that in a particular circumstance, at a given place and time, God is revealing himself supernaturally.

For instance, I do not doubt that God can directly and miraculously heal the sick according to his will. Almost every pastor has prayed for someone desperately ill and has seen them make a miraculous recovery. If that happens sometimes, why doesn't it happen all the time? Instead of blaming the sick for not having enough faith or the pastor for not being spiritual enough, the real answer, it seems to me, lies in the sovereignty of God. There are mysteries here that the human mind cannot fathom. Yet we are commanded to pray in faith, and so we do, believing that God will answer according to his will, sometimes in astonishing ways.

By the same token, I believe that God could use a dream or a vision to say something to us, his children, today. Although I tend to be cautious in this regard—both by nature and by theological background—it seems unwise to rule out any possibility of supernatural leading for the Christian today.

THE ROOF HANGS OVER THE EDGE

Several times in my own life I have felt God speaking directly to me. I don't mean that I heard an audible voice from God. I simply mean that something happened that I took to be a message from the Lord. Something of that nature happened during a visit to a mission station in Belize. Not surprisingly, it occurred during a period when I was going through a time of intense difficulty in my ministry. During the morning hours I taught the book of Romans to a group of eager students. Each night I would lie awake listening to the jungle sounds, my heart racing, my mind imagining one dire scenario after another. I tried to pray but found it incredibly difficult. Fear clutched at my heart, strangling my faith, squeezing out my confidence in God.

On Thursday morning I joined the staff prayer meeting. We began by listening quietly to what the Lord was saying to each of us individually. A missionary from New Zealand said that as an engineer the Lord usually spoke to him in visual images, not in specific words. He said that the Lord had told him to meditate on the small cabins where the workers lived. At first that puzzled him, but then he felt the Lord saying, "Look at the roofs on those cabins." The cabins are built with overhanging roofs because of the large amount of rainfall in Belize. Then the Lord said to him, "The cabin represents my people. The roof represents my protection. My people are worried that my protection won't stretch to the edges of their need. But they needn't worry. My protection is so vast, it goes far beyond their needs."

After sharing that, he looked around and said, "I don't know why God gave me that. There must be someone else who needs that message." The moment he said that, the Holy Spirit nudged me and said, "Ray, that was for you." Tears filled my eyes as I realized that God had brought me from Chicago to Belize at exactly the right moment when I needed to hear a message of hope from God.

Does that qualify as a supernatural experience? It does in my mind. I can't prove it in a court of law, but I have no doubt that God spoke directly to me at a moment of great personal need.

ONE NIGHT IN JUNE

I have had similar things happen a few other times in my life, although I don't know that I have had a truly supernatural vision. As I was preparing this chapter, my mind went back to the month after I graduated from high school. Like many other teenagers, I had no clear idea what to do with my life. Many people had urged me to consider going into the ministry, but I leaned toward a career in journalism. Late at night after everybody in our family had gone to bed, I paced back and forth in my bedroom. I was seventeen years old, about to leave home for the first time, thinking about my life and wondering what God wanted me to do. One night I had a dream in which I was preaching to a great multitude of people. I woke up and felt as if the dream had been sent by God to me. So I said, "All right, Lord, if you want me, I will be a preacher." No lights, no angelic voices, no music playing in the background. But that night changed my life. From that moment until now I have always believed that God called me to be a preacher of the Gospel.

Let me be clear at this point. That dream was not in the same category as Joseph's dream or Peter's vision. It may have been simply the logical result of all the days and weeks of pondering my future. Others may dismiss the whole thing as the product of adolescent imagination. But I can tell you that it actually happened to me. And it was a turning point in my life. As I write these words, I don't feel any particular need to defend myself. I simply pass along my own experience for your consideration. I have never heard God's voice speaking audibly to me, and I suppose that I would be filled with fear if I did. Nor do I seek such experiences. But why should it be thought strange that God would occasionally use unusual means to communicate encouragement and guidance to his children?

Before moving on, let me share one more story. This one doesn't come from my own experience. Greg and Carolyn Kirschner, missionary physicians serving in Nigeria, treated an infant boy who seemed to be healthy although he had briefly turned blue twice for no apparent reason. They hospitalized him primarily because his father had an intense dream in which his son became sick and died. After admitting the boy and checking him numerous times, they found nothing wrong. Then the boy experienced a prolonged seizure—something that was not medically expected. The father believes his dream saved his son's life. Writing about this episode, the missionaries commented how important dreams are in Nigerian culture. These highly-trained American physicians, having served in Nigeria for a decade, offer this observation:

> We have come to see that God definitely works through dreams in Nigeria. Many conversion stories here include two key elements: (1) An encounter with caring Christians who showed the love of Christ in a generous way; and (2) a dream or vision with a supernatural quality, most often involving an encounter with a "man in white."

I have heard similar things from other missionaries, especially those who work in predominately Muslim lands. Though this may sound strange to Westerners, we need not reject it outright. With appropriate safeguards regarding biblical authority, we can say that God may at times communicate in ways that appear to be supernatural.

FIVE CRUCIAL BIBLICAL TEXTS

With that as background let's look at five passages that will help us think biblically about this whole subject.

Numbers 12:6-8

> *If there is a prophet among you, I the LORD make myself known to him in a vision; I speak with him in a dream. Not so with my servant Moses. He is faithful in all my house. With him I speak mouth to mouth, clearly, and not in riddles.*

Notice the contrast in these verses. Prophets receive visions and dreams, but God spoke to Moses "clearly, and not in riddles."

Don't miss the point: *Dreams and visions are inherently ambiguous and difficult to understand.* When you have a dream, how do you know what it means? When you have a vision, you still have to interpret it. A dream or a vision is like a riddle. That's why there is a cottage industry in America that has grown up around dream interpretation. If you dream about a tree, how do you know what it means unless someone tells you? Otherwise you are just guessing.

Consider the case of a college student praying for guidance about being a foreign missionary. That afternoon he sees a cloud float overhead, and the cloud appears to be in the shape of Japan. So he concludes that God wants him to go to Japan. How do you know the cloud is supposed be Japan? How do you know it wasn't Vietnam? Or Argentina? It didn't say Japan. It just looked like Japan. Clouds change shape *every few seconds.* If he had looked two minutes later, he would have gone to Greenland. That's the point in Numbers 12:6-8. Even if you have a dream or a vision or a sign, it's ambiguous in and of itself. You can make it mean almost anything you want it to mean.

Psalm 119:105

Your word is a lamp to my feet and a light to my path.

Without God's Word we are left to our own unreliable devices. But when we let the light of the Bible shine upon our path, we are kept from falling into the ditch of foolish decisions. How often it happens that as we read the Bible on a daily basis, we discover that the passage we read in the morning was just what we needed for a situation we faced in the afternoon. God often fits his Word to the practical need of the moment. So out of the ancient prophecy of Micah or the practical words of Proverbs or the call to faithfulness in Hebrews 10 comes exactly the word from the Lord we need to hear.

Jeremiah 23:25-29

> I have heard what the prophets have said who prophesy lies in my name, saying, "I have dreamed, I have dreamed!" How long shall there be lies in the heart of the prophets who prophesy lies, and who prophesy the deceit of their own heart, who think to make my people forget my name by their dreams that they tell one another, even as their fathers forgot my name for Baal? Let the prophet who has a dream tell the dream, but let him who has my word speak my word faithfully. What has straw in common with wheat? declares the LORD. Is not my word like fire, declares the LORD, and like a hammer that breaks the rock in pieces?

This is a very solemn warning from God. False prophets constantly claim to have special messages from God. Like David Koresh of the Branch Davidians, or like Jim Jones of the People's Temple, they set themselves apart as having a direct line of communication with God. One way to spot a false prophet is to ask this simple question: *Does he believe that he has a special message from God, given only to him and not to anyone else?* When you hear a person make such a claim, beware. False prophets love to speak about their private communication with the Almighty. As Jeremiah says, they speak visions from "their own minds" (v. 26, NIV), spinning grandiose tales that come from their own overheated egos.

The warning is clear: Don't trust in dreams but in the written Word of God.

2 Timothy 3:16-17

> All Scripture is breathed out by God and profitable for teaching, for reproof, for correction, and for training in righteousness, that the man of God may be competent, equipped for every good work.

The key phrase is "breathed out by God." God literally breathed out the words of Scripture as he guided the minds of the Bible writers. That means that as Moses wrote the Pentateuch, God supernaturally guided the process so that as Moses wrote his words, he was also at the same time writing the very words God wanted written. The same is true for David, Isaiah, Luke, Paul, John, Peter, and all the other writers of Holy Scripture. What they wrote was truly theirs, based on their thought, their study, their insight, and was ultimately expressive of their own personality; yet it was at one and the same time *theopneustos*—God-breathed.

Why is this important? Notice the four purposes for the Word of God in verse 16. It is given to teach us, to rebuke us, to correct us, and to instruct us. Why? So that we may be equipped for everything God has for us to do. To be "equipped for every good work" carries with it the idea of being fully prepared so that no situation in life can catch you off guard. *There is something in the Bible to fit every case.* Whatever duty you have, whatever predicament you may find yourself in, the Word of God will equip you to face it with confidence.

The meaning is this: *God's Word is sufficient.* Nobody can add anything to it; nobody can take anything away from it. Build your life on the Word of God. Get your roots down into the Word of God. Find out what God has said in his Word, and you will discover his will for your life.

Here's a good test for those who think they have a vision from God. Check it out by the Bible. *If it contradicts or conflicts with the Word of God in any way, shape, or form, it is not from God, because God will not contradict himself.* He has already spoken in his Word. So check the vision or dream by the Word of God. Is it compatible with the Word of God? Does it reflect the will and Word of Jesus Christ? God's Word is the supreme standard for judging any vision, dream, or unusual circumstance.

1 Thessalonians 5:19-22

> Do not quench the Spirit [NIV, "do not put out the Spirit's fire"]. Do not despise prophecies, but test everything; hold fast what is good. Abstain from every form of evil.

These verses tucked away at the end of 1 Thessalonians are often overlooked, but they are actually quite instructive for our purposes. Here we have a balanced approach to the question of supernatural experiences. On the positive side, don't "quench the Spirit" or put out his fire. The Bible often uses the symbol of fire to picture the action of the Holy Spirit. Like a blazing fire, the Holy Spirit warms the heart, enlightens the mind, empowers the spirit, and burns away the dross of carnality. When the fire of the Spirit begins to move in a congregation, the results may be so supernatural that some believers may be tempted to "quench" the work of the Spirit.

How might that happen? First, *you might do it by stifling the Spirit's work in your own life.* That happens whenever you say no to God. Perhaps he is calling you to take a step of faith, to follow his divine guidance, to move out of your comfort zone, to exercise your spiritual gifts in a brand-new way, to demonstrate the reality of forgiveness and reconciliation in a broken relationship. Saying no in those situations is like throwing cold water on the fire of the Holy Spirit. Don't be surprised if your life then begins to grow cold.

Second, *you might do it by stopping the Spirit's work in someone else's life.* First Corinthians 12 speaks of various manifestations of the Holy Spirit. It speaks of differing operations and differing gifts. This can be a risky concept because we aren't all alike! God made you a unique creation. He gave you a combination of gifts, talents, and abilities that he gave to no one else in all the world. It's all too easy to become harsh and critical toward other believers who don't see things exactly as you do. It's perfectly legitimate to say that the Holy Spirit may work in your life differently than he may work in my life.

But that leads to a second question: Are we supposed to accept everything people say and do? The answer, of course, is no. To accept everything is to become naive and gullible. That is why Paul says, "Test everything; hold fast what is good. Abstain from every form of evil" (1 Thessalonians 5:21-22). The word "test" means to examine anything that purports to be from God to see if it is genuine. Hold fast to that which is good—i.e., in accordance with God's standard of truth. Reject everything that either appears to be evil or produces an evil result.

We might paraphrase 1 Thessalonians 5:19-22 in this way: "Be open to the work of the Spirit in the body through various gifted people. Examine everything carefully. Hold on to that which is good and true. Reject everything that is evil or produces evil." To the grumpy, supercritical believer who is closed to the work of the Spirit, God says, "Be open." To the gullible, untaught believer easily swayed by supposed supernaturalism, God says, "Be careful." A balanced approach says, "Let the Spirit move freely in your midst, and let everyone carefully examine the results."

This standard is not hard to apply. Suppose you watch some TV preacher who claims to have a message from God. Test it. What if somebody comes to you and says, "I have a message from God for you"? Test it. When a friend says, "I had a vision, and this is what I think God wants us to do," test it. That is what the Bible says. Test it. Don't put out the Spirit's fire. Don't despise what the prophets say. Test everything; hold on to the good; reject that which is evil.

A WORD OF CAUTION

Let me share a piece of advice with you. *Do not ever make a major decision in your life solely on the basis of what you believe to be a supernatural experience.* That's almost always a mistake. Don't get married just because you had a vision. Don't go to college just because you had a dream. Don't move to Japan because you saw it floating overhead in the clouds. Don't kiss a young woman just because the fish were kissing each other. You'll get in trouble that way. Don't make a major decision in your life solely on the basis of that which appears to you to be supernatural.

THE FOUR-WAY TEST

Here's a simple four-way test for anything that appears to be a supernatural message from God to you:

The Test of Scripture

Test it by the Word of God. Many foolish decisions would be avoided if we simply applied what God has already said about the situation at hand. For instance, you don't need to pray about marrying an unbeliever because God has already told us his will in this area (2 Corinthians 6:14). Nor do we need to wonder if it is God's will for us to show compassion to the poor. You only need to read Proverbs 19:17 and 21:13. How should we respond to those who hurt us deliberately? Ponder the words of Jesus in Luke 6:27-31. What if you think God wants you to commit suicide? Before you pull the trigger, read Exodus 20:13, Deuteronomy 30:19, and John 10:10. Sometimes we struggle to discover what we call "God's will," but we forget that the Bible is a book filled with God's will. Through commands, precepts, proverbs, and abundant examples, it teaches us what the will of God is. Are you tempted to indulge in ingratitude? Read 1 Thessalonians 5:18. Do you delude yourself that God isn't bothered when you look at pornography? Memorize Matthew 5:28.

This list of examples could be extended almost indefinitely. God's Word speaks to every situation of life. You will never encounter a situation to which the Bible does not speak either in terms of direct command or general precept. That's the first test for any supposed supernatural experience: Is it consistent with what God has said in his Word?

The Test of Time

Let's suppose you get a supernatural sign of some kind. *Wait before you make a major decision.* Wait a day. Wait a week. Wait a month. If it's from God, it will still be from God next week. If it's from God, it will still be from God a month from now. Don't be afraid to wait for the Lord to send further confirmation.

The Test of Counsel

Proverbs 19:20 offers this wisdom about receiving advice: "Listen to advice and accept instruction, that you may gain wisdom in the future." *As a general rule, God will rarely speak to you in such a way that no one else around you recognizes it as the voice of God.* If it is truly of God, other spiritual men and women normally will recognize it as well.

The Test of Confirmation

If you have a dream or a vision or some other unusual event that seems like a message from God, ask him to confirm it by non-supernatural means. Ask God to show you biblical principles that line up with your experience. Search the Word for his instruction. Spend time in prayer with others. Seek godly counsel. Wait on the Lord. Spend a day fasting before the Lord. Set aside time for extended prayer. Keep a journal of your thoughts and insights. Search for confirming circumstances. If your dream is from God, he will be glad to confirm it for you. Don't make a major decision until you have received that confirmation from other sources.

FIVE PRACTICAL CONCLUSIONS

Let's wrap up this chapter with five practical conclusions. What are we to do about dreams, visions, and supernatural signs? Here are five pieces of advice for you.

Don't Rule Them Out

Although I tend to be very skeptical about many supposed supernatural revelations, I don't think we should go to the opposite extreme and rule them out altogether. Why run the risk of putting out the Spirit's fire? There's a danger that we will become so rigid in our faith that we unconsciously say, "God, you can only speak to us *this* way. You can't speak to us *that* way." He's God. He can speak to us any way he desires.

Don't Seek Them

Don't seek supernatural signs. This is where people get in trouble. *They attempt to make commonplace that which is by definition very rare.* Many Christians never have a supernatural experience of any kind. It doesn't matter. You are not a less spiritual Christian if these things don't happen to you. I wouldn't recommend that anyone ask God for a vision or some other supernatural event. If God wants to communicate to you that way, he can do so at any time. By seeking such things you may be opening yourself to false spiritual experiences. And you may be setting yourself up for a fall if God doesn't meet your expectations.

Don't Try to Force God's Hand

Some people try to force God to give them a miracle. They think that by doing certain things they can cause God to respond in certain ways. "Lord, I'm going to fast until you send me a supernatural sign." It's usually a mistake to try something like that. You may end up starving to death. The Bible warns against putting God to the test; that is, don't attempt to usurp God's rightful place as the Sovereign Lord of the universe.

Stay in Touch with the Holy Spirit

Stay open to the Spirit's working in your life. He wants to guide your life moment by moment. Let him guide you in any way he sees fit. The Lord rarely leads us in the same way every time. *Above all, make sure you are filled with the Spirit, so he has free reign in your life.* The issue is not supernatural signs, but being so yielded to the Lord that you are fully responsive to the Lord's work in your life.

Build Your Life on the Word of God

Don't make the mistake of building your spiritual life on signs and wonders. God never meant for you to be a miracle junkie, rushing from one emotional high to another. What will you do when the miracles stop coming? Or your dreams become ordinary? Or the clouds stop looking like Japan? Or the fish stop kissing each other? Or the roof no longer hangs over the edge of the cabin?

There is only one solid foundation for your life—the Word of God.

Can God work miracles today? Yes. Does he? I believe the answer is yes. Might he work a miracle in your life or communicate his will to you in some unusual way? I think the answer is yes to all those things. Certainly God often answers our prayers in ways that are beyond human understanding. But our greatest need is not for more miracles but to know the awesome God who reveals himself to us in the Bible. As we learn more about him through the Word of God, we will build our lives on a foundation that can never fail.

You may have dreams, visions, and supernatural signs, or you may not. It doesn't matter one way or the other. *Build your life upon the Word of God.* When you come to the end, you will not be disappointed but will be delighted to discover that God has kept his word to you.

QUESTIONS FOR PERSONAL/GROUP STUDY

1. Would you like to have a dream or vision or supernatural sign? Would that encourage your faith if you knew it came from God? Why or why not?
2. Have you ever had a dream or vision that seemed to contain some message from God to you? Describe it. What decisions (if any) did you make on the basis of what you felt God said to you? What principles should a person use in evaluating such an experience?
3. Do you believe that if you had more faith you would see more miracles in your life? Why or why not?
4. Do you agree with the statement that "you should never make a major decision solely on the basis of a supposed supernatural sign from God"? What are some potential dangers?
5. What are the dangers of *seeking* messages from God through dreams, visions, and supernatural signs?
6. Why is it important that we build our lives upon God's Word? Name three ways to do that.

GOING DEEPER

Out of the blue you receive a call from your best friend's wife, asking for your help. Her husband heard God speak to him in a dream telling him to move to Alaska and start an Internet pottery exchange. Now he is in the process of selling their home so they can move to Alaska and start the new business. You've never known your friend to do anything like this before. His wife asks you to intervene, knowing that her husband will listen to you. When you get together, he tells his story and then waits for your response. What questions will you ask? What Scriptures will you cite? What advice will you give to your best friend?

5

How to Make a
Tough Decision

*Trust in the LORD with all your heart, and do not lean on your
own understanding. In all your ways acknowledge him, and
he will make straight your paths. (Proverbs 3:5-6)*

These two verses are among the most beloved in the entire
Bible. You may have memorized them in Sunday school
when you were a child. Or perhaps you made a cross-stitch pattern of these words and hung it on your wall. Or you may have
learned to sing these words as part of a contemporary worship
chorus. British Bible teacher G. Campbell Morgan said that when
he was leaving home for the first time, his father pressed a note
into his hand. When Campbell Morgan unfolded it, he discovered
it contained just one verse of Scripture: "In all thy ways acknowledge him, and he shall direct thy paths." Looking back years later,
he noted that his father had written that verse with no accompa-
nying comment. No comment, he said, except the comment of his
father's godly life.

This text is striking in its simplicity. There is nothing difficult about it. It is so simple that it can be understood by the youngest believer, and yet it is a comfort to the oldest saint of God. And it is good for everyone in between. These words cling to the soul because they speak to a great need we all feel—the need for guidance. Proverbs 3:5-6 suggests the basis on which guidance will come. *It is a short course in knowing God's will for your life.* If you learn what this passage is teaching and begin to apply it to your daily life, it will make a profound difference when you need to make a tough decision.

I am beginning this chapter with the assumption that some of us have known these verses for a long time. Sometimes when we know a passage so well, we almost know it too well. We have heard it so often that we have never stopped to think about what it is really saying. Familiarity can breed contempt. You may even be thinking, "I already know this verse—maybe I'll skip to the last chapter." Please don't do that. I want you to capture the truth of Proverbs 3:5-6 in a fresh way.

FIVE KEY WORDS

Not long ago I had a chance to study these verses in depth for the first time. As I did, I discovered that five key words unlock the message of this text. Let's take those key words one by one and see what each one teaches us.

Trust

"*Trust* in the LORD with all your heart." In our thinking the word *trust* means to rely upon or to have confidence in. But the Hebrew word is stronger. The word translated "trust" means "to lean with the full body," "to lay upon." It has the idea of stretching yourself out upon a bed or resting on a hard surface. The word means to put your full weight on something. *To trust in the Lord is to rest your whole weight upon him*—to depend on him completely.

Lean

"Do not *lean* on your own understanding." To lean means to rest upon something for partial support. Leaning is what you do when you walk with a cane or hold on to a walker because you are unsteady. The Hebrew word is used for leaning against a tree or a stone cliff. You lean on something when you are not strong enough to stand alone.

Understanding

"Do not lean on your own *understanding*." "Understanding" refers to the mental processes by which you analyze a problem, break it down into its smaller parts, and then make a decision about what you are going to do. Early in the morning when you make a list of all the things you have to do that day, you use your understanding to sort out your priorities. Or it's what you use on Sunday night when you map out the upcoming week. That's understanding. You use it any time you plan your life or solve a problem. Understanding is the decision-making ability that God has given you.

When you take the word "lean" and bring in the idea of "understanding," then add the negative, the meaning is some-thing like this: "Use all your mental powers, but do not lean on them for total support." Don't trust in your own ability to figure out your life. Lean instead on the Lord! Rest your weight on him!

Acknowledge

"In all your ways *acknowledge* him." This word deserves extra consideration because the word "acknowledge" can be hard to understand. In the Hebrew this word is an imperative—a com-mand. You could translate this by saying, "In all your ways *know* him." The Hebrew word means to know deeply and intimately.

It's the kind of knowing that comes with personal experience. It means to know something through and through. For instance, somebody might say, "Do you know the President of the United States?" I would say, "Sure, I know the President." If the President walked in the room, I would know who he is. If I heard his voice coming over the TV, I would recognize it. Or if I saw his picture on the front page of the newspaper, I would know it was the President.

Now, I don't really *know* him. I can't pick up the phone and call the White House and say, "Mr. President, this is Ray Pritchard. Let's do lunch this week." He won't take my call because I don't know him personally. I just know him at the level of head knowledge. I don't know him intimately or on a friendship level.

There is another kind of knowing. My wife and I know each other in a completely different way. We've known each other intimately for over thirty years. After being together that long, strange things begin to happen. I will be sitting in the car thinking about a song—and she'll start singing it. How does that happen? I don't know. Or I will be thinking about a question, and before I can ask it, she'll blurt out the answer. How does she do that? I don't know. Or I'll start a sentence, and to my great consternation she will finish the sentence before I do. When I say, "How can you do that?" she says with a smile, "I know what you are thinking even before you say it."

Things like that happen to all married couples eventually. When you live together for many years, you get to know each other at such a deep level that you actually begin to know what the other person is thinking even as he or she is thinking it. You know what your wife is going to say before she says it. You know what your husband is going to do before he does it. You have a deep, personal, intimate knowledge of each other.

Seen in that light, we might translate verse 5 this way: "In all your ways know God intimately . . . deeply . . . personally. When you know God that way in every area of your life, he will direct your paths."

Direct

That brings me to the fifth word, which in the King James Version is translated, "He shall *direct* thy paths." That isn't bad. But I think the ESV translation is a little better: "He will make straight your paths." Imagine that you are driving along a road that appears to be impassable. The road winds through the mountains and down into the swamps. It seems to have a thousand switchbacks. As you travel on, you discover that portions of the road are washed out, others are filled with potholes, and still others are blocked by huge boulders. In some places the road apparently becomes a dead-end.

This is the road of your life. As you look at it, it appears to be covered with boulders and rocks. Some parts of it seem to be filled with potholes; other sections appear to be going nowhere. That's the way life is.

Here is God's message to you from Proverbs 3:5-6. *If you will know God in every area of your life, he will take personal responsibility to make your way smooth and straight.* He will remove the obstacles if they need to be removed. He will fill in the potholes if they need to be filled. He will redirect the detour so that what seemed to be a dead-end turns out to be the shortest way to reach your destination.

All you have to do is trust in the Lord. Lay yourself completely on him for full support. Don't lean on your own human understanding. In all your ways know God intimately. He will take the path of your life that seems to go up and down and around and sometimes seems to curve backwards, and he will make your way straight. That's the promise of Almighty God to you.

PHILIP YANCEY'S DEFINITION

But it won't always be easy or come quickly. For most of us, most of the time, the exact opposite will be true. Discovering God's will takes time as the events of life unfold before us, often in ways that seem to make no sense at all. Rarely will we know the whole plan in advance. And as I've already pointed out, that's actually a good thing. I wrote the first edition of this book ten years ago. As I sit at my computer and ponder the course of my life over the last decade, I find it easier to recall the hard times than the good times.

I remember a painful controversy in the church that led to broken friendships and misunderstanding. A very close friend died suddenly and without warning. My youngest son went through a harrowing medical crisis that threatened his life, and in various forms it continues to this day. But that's only one side of the ledger. In the last decade our three boys graduated from high school, the oldest graduated from college, the middle son graduates in a few months, and our youngest son is currently in college. I am blessed with a wife with amazing gifts who still loves me after thirty years of marriage. I still serve the same church and am surrounded by very capable leaders. My health is good. So what do I have to complain about? Not much at all. Ten years ago I had no clue what the next decade would hold. Looking back, I'm happy that I didn't know anything in advance.

My favorite definition of faith comes from Philip Yancey who said, "Faith means believing in advance what will only make sense in reverse." We want to know why things happen the way they do and why couldn't things have happened some other way. It would be wrong to say that faith provides all the answers. It doesn't. Perhaps in heaven we will fully understand, or in heaven our desire to know will be transformed by our vision of the Lord. By faith we see things that are invisible to others, and by faith we believe in advance those things that right now make no sense but one day will make perfect sense because we will view them in reverse.

The world says, "Seeing is believing." God says, "Believing is seeing." We believe; therefore we see.

WHEN YOU NEED TO KNOW, YOU'LL KNOW

I saw this principle in action several years ago when a young couple, recently graduated from Moody Bible Institute, came to see me. They had just finished the first part of a training course with a missions organization in the Chicago area. Their advisor told them they needed to talk with their pastor before making the next step. So they came to see me with the good news that God was calling them to the mission field. "Where do you want to go?" I asked. "We don't know," the husband replied. So I looked at the wife, and she smiled in agreement. "You mean you have no idea at all?" "No idea at all." I held up my hand and moved it as if I were twirling a globe. "You mean that in all the world, you don't have even a tiny idea where you would like to go?" "No." That does make it difficult when you are trying to raise funds because they couldn't answer the first question: "Where do you plan to go?"

I sat there silently for a moment, pondering the situation. No one had ever said anything like that to me before. Suddenly I had a flash of inspiration. Looking right at that young couple, I said, "I've got the answer. The reason you don't know is because you don't need to know because if you needed to know, you would know, but since you don't know, you must not need to know, because if you had needed to know by now, you would know by now, but since you don't know, you must not need to know because when you need to know, you'll know. If God is God, that must be true." They were dazzled and speechless, and I was pretty amazed myself because all of that just came popping out at the spur of the moment. We prayed, and they left my office, still smiling.

Not long after that, I happened to meet a young lady from our church who was working at Moody Bible Institute. She had a job in the music library that was scheduled to come to an end in a few months. Our paths crossed in the sanctuary lobby between services. When I asked her what she planned to do next, she said she had no idea. So on the spur of the moment I decided to try it again. "The reason you don't know is because you don't need to know because if you needed to know, you would know, but since you don't know, you must not need to know, because if you had needed to know by now, you would know by now, but since you don't know, you must not need to know because when you need to know, you'll know. If God is God, that must be true." She laughed and said that sounded right. And off she went.

Several weeks later when I saw her again, she had a big smile on her face. "Pastor Ray, you won't believe what happened. I was talking with a friend about things, and my friend asked me if I had ever considered going to the mission field. I said no, and she said I should think about it. But I'm a music librarian. What would I do on the mission field? But a few days later I happened to pass by a missions display and saw a representative sitting there. Normally I would just walk right by, but this time I stopped to talk. When I asked if they ever needed librarians on the mission field, the man said, 'Absolutely! We could use some librarians right now.' So I started doing some research, and on a website I discovered a Christian school in Kenya that needed a librarian starting exactly when I finish my job at Moody. I e-mailed them, they e-mailed back, and they checked my references. And guess what, Pastor Ray? I got the job! I'm moving to Nairobi, Kenya, to get started as the librarian for a Christian school." As I write these words, she is finishing her fourth year there and is extremely happy in her work.

Not long after that, the young couple came back to see me with similar good news. "We're going to Russia." "No kidding. Russia. That's great. Did you know about this when you came to see me?" "No, we had no idea." "So where in Russia are you going?" "We're going to the Black Sea." "That's fantastic. What are you going to do there?" "We're going to teach in a school and help with church planting." When I asked them how they ended up going to the Black Sea to teach and do church planting, they told me a story that was so detailed that it was positively Byzantine in its complexity.

They met someone who knew someone who "happened" to know a woman whom they met almost by chance. She came over to talk to them, and one thing led to another, and now they were going to Russia. I couldn't draw it on a chart if I tried. But they were so happy about it, and I was happy for them. They are currently involved in their ministry near the Black Sea teaching and helping plant churches.

I am amazed as I think about how God led that young woman and that young couple to Kenya and Russia respectively. But on second thought, why be amazed? That's how God works, isn't it? When you need to know, you'll know. Not one day sooner, not one day later. And if today you don't know what to do next, it's because you truly don't need to know. Because if you needed to know, you would know. If God is God, that must be true.

That's why the search for God's will is so exhilarating. When God is leading the way, every obstacle will eventually be removed. The path may have many twists and turns, but in the end he will make your path straight. You have his word on it.

"BLESS IT ALL, LORD"

So many people struggle at this very point. The Bible says, in all your ways know God intimately, know him deeply, know him personally. As a man knows a woman—know God that way. Know him to that depth. Know him with that kind of intimacy. So often we skip this. When we get up in the morning, we say, "O God, help me. I'm busy today. I've got so much to do. Lord, I don't even have time to pray—so here's my list. Bless it all, Lord. I've got to go." We throw our list up toward heaven while we run out the door. What we are saying is, "God, here's my schedule. Please rubber-stamp it with your blessing." And we wonder why our days are filled with frustration.

Many of us go through life leaning almost completely on our own understanding. We like to be in control. I number myself among that group. I like to know what's going on. I like to be in charge of my own destiny. This passage is a warning to all of us who lay out life the way we want it and then say, "Here, God, stamp it with your blessing because I am going to go out and do it for you." God says, "I don't work that way. Know me first. Put me first in everything, including all your plans, all your thinking, and all your scheming. Put me first, and I then will make your way straight."

WE WANT A FORMULA—GOD WANTS A RELATIONSHIP

Do you want to know the secret of knowing the will of God? Here it is: *In everything you do, know God*. But we all want a formula. "I don't like that. Give me a formula. Give me three steps." Proverbs 3:5-6 tells us that the secret is a *relationship* with God. Let's talk about Joe, who has been dating Shirley for nine months. When he picks her up for their Friday night date, she asks the logical question: "Where are we going tonight?" "I don't know. I want to take you someplace you like. I wish you would give me a three-step formula so I could know where you really want to go on Friday nights." How would Shirley feel? Angry, upset, frustrated. "How is it that we've been dating every week for nine months and you don't know what I like and don't like? Where have you been all this time?" She would have a right to be angry.

We want to reduce our relationship with God to a formula. But God says, "Know me. Spend time with me. Put me first in every area of your life because when you do that, I will take care of all those details." This is a revolutionary way of looking at life.

Minnesota or South Carolina?

We're hung up on the decisions of life. Should I go here? Should I go there? Should I live in Minnesota? Should I live in South Carolina? Should I marry Jane or Sue or Ellen or Sherry? Should I take the job, or should I say no? Here is the teaching of this passage stated in one sentence: *God is much less concerned with what you do than with what kind of person you are.* So when you say, "Lord, should I go to Minnesota or should I go to South Carolina?" you are asking the wrong question. The question is not where are you going to go, but what kind of person you are going to be wherever you go. The question is not, who should I marry, but what kind of person am I going to be no matter whom I marry?

While you are wrestling with the question of relocation, God wants to know, "Are you going to be my man or my woman whether you go to Minnesota or South Carolina or whether you stay in Santa Fe?" If you decide to put God first in everything, it doesn't matter where you live. And if you are not going to put God first in everything, it doesn't matter where you live either. We focus all our energy on decisions. But God says, "Know me, and I will take care of the details." We want specific direction.

God says, "In all your ways know me, and everything else will fall into place."

WHAT DIFFERENCE WILL IT MAKE IN TEN THOUSAND YEARS?

A few years ago I heard someone say that most of our decisions won't matter at all in ten thousand years. That blew my mind at first. What a liberating way to look at life. The next time you face a tough decision, ask yourself, will it really matter in ten thousand years? Ninety-nine percent of what you worried about this week won't matter three weeks from now, much less ten thousand years from now. In the year 2452 it won't matter whether you lived in Minnesota, New Mexico, or South Carolina. But what will matter is that you have decided in all your ways to know God. That is what will really matter. All these trivial, piddly details that just soak up so much energy will in that day be seen for what they really are—trivial, piddly details.

In light of this text, what is the will of God for your life? *To know God in everything. To see him present everywhere and in everything, and to live in total surrender to him.* The most important thing is not the decisions you face; the most important thing is your relationship with God. And the closer you get to God, the easier it will be for God to guide you in the way he wants you to go.

"LORD, HERE ARE MY HANDS"

Knowing God means using all your energies for him.

> *Lord, here are my hands.*
> *Lord, here are my lips.*
> *Lord, here are my eyes.*
> *Lord, here are my ears.*
> *Lord, here are my feet.*

Knowing God means taking all that you have and placing it at the disposal of the King of kings and the Lord of lords. Proverbs 3:5-6 ends with a promise: "He will make straight your paths." God is able to remove the obstacles in front of you. He is able to fill in the potholes and turn a dead-end into a four-lane highway. *God rewards those who show regard for him by leading them straight to the right end and removing all the obstacles along the way.*

We rarely see this in advance. We mostly see the potholes. The boulders block our view. Many times it seems as if there is no path at all. But he will make a way. No one can say how he will do it. There are thousands of ways in which God leads his children. He leads us through delays, detours, miracles, the advice of friends, unexpected opportunities, suddenly closed doors, answered prayer, unanswered prayer, inner impressions, and a still, small voice in the night.

You don't see it on this side. On this side you see the problems. But when you know God, he leads you step by step. When the journey is done, you will look back and say, "I don't know how I got from there to here, but I do know this: Jesus led me all the way."

"HOW DID I GET HERE?"

A friend of ours used those very words to describe a months-long ordeal that involved a change of jobs, a cross-country move, and a total redirection of her life. As the time drew near, the emotional stress of leaving the familiar for the unknown almost overwhelmed her. I think she would probably say that making this particular move was the single most difficult thing she has ever had to do. All along the way she was torn with inner doubts—wanting to do the right thing, but not sure if she was. When I saw her around a campfire one night there were tears in her eyes. "Am

I doing the right thing? I'm not sure." Then two weeks later she took a deep breath and moved to her new home. Just before leaving, she made an interesting comment: "How did I get here? In my heart I believe I'm doing the right thing, but looking back I'm not sure how I got from Point A to Point B. Only God could have done it because I never would have done it myself." But she smiled when she said it.

Doing God's will often involves great uncertainty and periods of deep doubt. But if you are willing to do what he wants you to do, he then takes responsibility to reach into the chaos of life and lead you step by step to the place where he wants you to be.

THE TWENTY-ONE-DAY CHALLENGE

My wife and I had lunch with friends who were visiting from a distant city. As we began our meal, the thought passed through my mind that the husband looked more relaxed than I had seen him in a long time. I soon discovered the reason for his calm demeanor. He told me about a simple prayer he had been praying at the beginning of each new day. He heard a noted Christian leader suggest using this prayer for twenty-one days. My friend said that he had tried it and that the prayer had made a profound difference in his life. At that point his wife chimed in to say that she had noticed a drastic difference in him as well.

Before he started praying that prayer, he often came home tense over things that had happened to him during the day. But now he comes home relaxed and in a good mood. As I listened, I wondered to myself what kind of magic prayer could make that kind of difference. My friend said that for him the key is to pray the prayer the moment he wakes up—even before he gets out of bed. He even said that he had awakened that morning at 4:30 A.M., so he prayed the prayer and then went back to sleep.

The prayer itself is the essence of simplicity. It goes like this:

"Heavenly Father, you are in charge of everything that will happen to me today—whether it be good or bad, positive or negative. Please make me thankful for everything that happens to me today. Amen."

This prayer is powerful because it doesn't change anything outside of me, but it does change everything inside of me. My circumstances don't change, but my attitude does. And that's why my friend looked so relaxed when we ate lunch.

Perhaps you need to take the twenty-one-day challenge. Take that simple prayer and pray it first thing in the morning for the next twenty-one days and see what happens in your heart.

Life is a mysterious journey, full of unexpected twists and turns. The path ahead is a mystery to us all. No one can say for sure what is around the next bend. It may be a smooth road through a lovely valley, or we may discover that the bridge is washed out and we have to find a way to cross a deep river. Often the road will seem to disappear, or it may suddenly seem to go in three different directions, and we won't know which way to go. But there is One who knows the way because the past, present, and future are all the same to him, and the darkness is as the light of day to him. He knows the way we should go. He has promised to direct your path, and he will do it. You can count on it.

QUESTIONS FOR PERSONAL/GROUP STUDY

1. Proverbs 3:5 says, "Do not lean on your own understanding." Yet God gave you a mind, that you might use it wisely. How can you use the understanding God has given you without leaning on it for total support?

2. Everyone trusts in something. What are the distinguishing marks of a person who is truly trusting in the Lord? How can you pick such a person out of a crowd?

3. Why does discovering God's will often involve periods of confusion and personal chaos?

4. How do you feel about the statement that "God is more interested in *who* you are than in *where* you are"? Does that mean it's wrong to seek guidance about where you live? Whenever you face a big decision, what priority should be even bigger than making the right choice?

5. Take a look at your own life. What are you doing right now to know God intimately?

6. Do you feel confident about your own future? Why or why not? As you think about that question, where does God enter the picture?

GOING DEEPER

This chapter mentions a prayer that someone prayed as part of a twenty-one-day challenge: "Heavenly Father, you are in charge of everything that will happen to me today—whether it be good or bad, positive or negative. Please make me thankful for everything that happens to me today. Amen." Try praying this prayer first thing in the morning for the next three weeks, and see what difference it makes in your life.

6

THE MOST IMPORTANT INGREDIENT

When was the last time you played with modeling clay? It may have been a while unless you have a house full of preschoolers. As all parents know, children love modeling clay because they can make almost anything with it. When it first comes out of the can, the clay feels cold and clammy and mushy. It's bendable and easily made into any one of a 1,001 different shapes. You can take modeling clay and make a little baseball with it. Or you can make it flat like a piecrust. If you like, you can roll it up and make a baseball bat. Or you can take that thing that looks like a bat and bend it into the shape of a little horse. Then you can turn the horse into a rabbit or a pig, depending on how fat you make it. You can do anything you like when the modeling clay is soft.

WANTED: BENDABLE BELIEVERS

But what happens to the modeling clay when you leave it out for three days? It dries up and becomes hard and brittle. When you try to shape it, you can't because it's not soft any longer. *There*

107

are many Christians who are like that before the Lord. They are hard, brittle, and unbendable. They are set in their ways, with their own plans, their own agendas, their own desires.

Christians like that wonder why guidance is hard to find. But it's really not hard to understand. When your life becomes hard and brittle before the Lord, God speaks, but you don't hear. He leads, but you don't follow. He opens doors, but you refuse to enter. That is why there is no principle more important than the principle of being able to be guided, being soft and bendable in the hands of God so he can shape you the way he wants.

We find many examples of this in the Bible:

Samuel said, "Speak, for your servant hears" (1 Samuel 3:10).

David said, "Teach me your way, O LORD" (Psalm 27:11).

Solomon said, "In all your ways acknowledge him" (Proverbs 3:6).

Isaiah said, "Here am I! Send me" (Isaiah 6:8).

Saul (Paul) said, "What shall I do, Lord?" (Acts 22:10).

All that I have written so far can be wrapped up in one sentence: *Guidable people always receive guidance from God.* Why is that? Because God always speaks loud enough for a willing ear to hear. Therefore, there is nothing more important than being open to receive guidance from God.

How will you find the guidance you need? In one sense that's a tough question because God speaks to us in a variety of ways. We may hear a sermon, read a passage of Scripture, receive advice from our friends, feel some inner sense of direction, or have doors of opportunity open or close.

A MOST UNLIKELY TEXT

There is a marvelous passage in the book of Acts that pictures for us some of the major ways in which God guides his children. Acts 16:6-10 tells the story of Paul and Silas at the beginning of their second missionary journey. They had joined forces to visit the churches, preach the Word, and strengthen the saints. As we shall see, their travel plans changed several times. Luke paints the picture in these five insightful verses:

> *And they went through the region of Phrygia and Galatia, having been forbidden by the Holy Spirit to speak the word in Asia. And when they had come up to Mysia, they attempted to go into Bithynia, but the Spirit of Jesus did not allow them. So, passing by Mysia, they went down to Troas. And a vision appeared to Paul in the night: a man of Macedonia was standing there, urging him and saying, "Come over to Macedonia and help us." And when Paul had seen the vision, immediately we sought to go on into Macedonia, concluding that God had called us to preach the gospel to them.*

You could read this text 150 times and you might say, "I don't see anything in there about discovering the will of God." Yet this little slice of life from the first century shows us how God's will may be discovered in the ordinary affairs of life. What happened to them often happens to us. So then, how does guidance come? This text reveals four answers to that question.

Answer #1:
Guidance comes through obedience in the ordinary

Verse 6 tells us that "they went through the region of Phrygia and Galatia, having been forbidden by the Holy Spirit to speak the word in Asia." *Paul was on a mission from God to preach the Gospel.* That's the one motivating factor that explains his life. That's why he made one hazardous journey after another. He determined to go wherever he could to spread the good news about Jesus Christ. The only thing that Paul didn't know was exactly where he was going to do it. The guidance he needed concerned *where* to preach, not *whether* to preach. He would continue preaching wherever he found himself.

99 PERCENT OF LIFE

That leads to a profound insight: *99 percent of life is ordinary.* It's just the same old stuff day after day. You get up in the morning, take a shower, put your clothes on, eat breakfast, get the kids ready for school, go to work, hope the kids are OK, come back from work dead-tired, read the paper, watch TV, try to be nice, eat supper, play with the kids, flop into bed dead-tired, then get up the next morning and do it all over again. That's the way life is. It's the same old thing day after day.

Where do you begin in discovering the will of God? *You begin by doing what you already know to be the will of God in your present situation.* So many of us live for those mountain-peak experiences, those times when the clouds part and God seems so close to us.

GET UP AND DO IT!

Many people wish those spectacular moments would happen every day. Often when we say, "God, show me your will," what we really mean is, "Lord, give me some feeling, some insight, some spiritual revelation." And God says, "I have already shown you my will. Now just get up and do it!"

- What is God's will for a student? God's will for a student is to do his/her homework.
- What is God's will for a doctor? Get up and do your rounds early in the morning.
- What is God's will for a pharmacist? Take extra care as you fill those prescriptions.

- What is God's will for a banker? Take care of the money entrusted to you.
- What is God's will for an accountant? Take care of those books, and do the job right.
- What is God's will for a teacher? Do your lesson plans, and come to class ready to teach.
- What is God's will for a salesman? Know your product, make your contacts, and move the merchandise.
- What is God's will for a football coach? Get your team ready to play the big game on Friday night.
- What is God's will for an assembly-line worker? Show up on time, sober, with a good attitude, ready to work.
- What is God's will for a flight attendant? Be on time, in uniform, with a smile on your face.

If you are a young mother and want to know what God's will is, it has something to do with dirty diapers. God's will for young mothers is *more* than dirty diapers, but it's not *less* than that. God's will for a secretary is *more* than typing, but it's not *less* than that. God's will for you is *more* than showing up and doing a job, but it is not *less* than that.

So many of us want to live only on the mountaintop. That's not where you discover God's will. *You discover God's will in the nitty-gritty of the valley every single day.* The Bible says, "Whatever your hand finds to do, do it with your might" (Ecclesiastes 9:10). Why should God show you his will for the future if you aren't doing the will of God in the present?

That's all-important. What do preachers do? They preach. And that's what you see in Acts 16—preachers who are willing to preach anytime they get the opportunity. They are just looking for the right open door. Because they are willing to obey what they know to be the will of God, God is therefore free to show them the next step.

WHAT DALLAS WILLARD TOLD MY FRIEND

I have a pastor friend who a few years back struck up a friendship with best-selling Christian author Dallas Willard. They met at a conference where Willard was speaking. After the conference my friend wrote Dallas Willard a letter and eventually received a cordial reply. He wrote him once or twice more over the course of several years. My friend came to a crisis point in his ministry and went away on a personal retreat to consider what he should do. He faced some opposition in his congregation and wondered if the time had come to seek another church. So he sat down and poured out his heart in a long letter.

When my friend described the letter to me, it sounded as if he had written many pages, going into great detail about the various problems he faced and the people who were giving him trouble. I pause here to say that we all think about writing letters like that from time to time, but most of us never actually do it. But my friend did, and when he dropped the letter in the mailbox, he immediately thought, *That was a mistake. Dallas Willard is a very busy man, he probably gets lots of mail, and who am I to write him with all my problems?* All very true, by the way. But the letter was already in the mail.

So my friend waited for a few days, feeling bad about having poured out his problems to someone he didn't know that well. But after a week or two or three, when no answer came, he felt worse because he thought surely he had offended a man he greatly respected. A longer time passed, a month or two, so long that he had concluded that he would never receive a reply. Then one day he was surprised to receive a letter in the mail from Dallas Willard. The envelope was light—there was only one sheet of paper inside. And the answer to the many pages of problems, worries, fears, and confusion came in just two sentences: "Thank you for writing. I think you should just get up every day and do what you believe God wants you to do and stop worrying so much about what other people think." That was it. That plus the salutation and the "Yours in Christ, Dallas Willard."

What did my friend think? He loved the reply. It was exactly what he needed to hear. Dallas Willard was right—and his advice applies to all of us. If you don't know what else to do tomorrow morning, just get up and do what you believe God wants you to do—and don't worry about what other people think. That's not an infallible rule, but it's pretty good—and it covers 99 percent of our tomorrows. God's will begins with obedience in the ordinary.

The Acts passage reveals a second principle about how guidance comes to us.

Answer #2:
Guidance comes through suddenly changing circumstances

Paul and his team wanted to go east into Asia, but the Holy Spirit prevented them. Question: How did the Holy Spirit do that? I have no idea. It could have been the result of various circumstances preventing them. Perhaps the road was washed out, or perhaps there was Jewish opposition so they couldn't get in. The Holy Spirit could have communicated through an inner impression or even a voice from God. A prophet might have delivered the message. No one knows how it happened. But somehow they knew they were not to go east.

So instead they went north toward Bithynia. Why? They intended to preach the Gospel there. They still had the same purpose—to preach the Gospel; only now it was redirected through suddenly changing circumstances. But as they tried to enter

Bithynia, "the Spirit of Jesus did not allow them." Another mystery. The Bible doesn't explain how this happened. But somehow they knew the Spirit of Jesus was saying no. I tend to think that as they were praying, they had a strong impression from the Lord, or perhaps someone received a prophecy. But that's only speculation. Somehow the Lord made it clear: "Don't go to Bithynia." So they headed west to preach the Gospel and ended up in a place called Troas.

HAS GOD MADE A MISTAKE?

What was going on here? *God was revealing his will through suddenly changing circumstances.* Have you ever had that happen to you? You had your life all planned out. You were going *this* way. You were convinced that God's will was *this* way. Then the phone call came that changed the course of your life. Or the boss called you in and said, "We're downsizing. Your job has been eliminated." Or the letter came that said, "You are an excellent candidate, but unfortunately our incoming class is full." Or you asked her to marry you, knowing it was the will of God, but she hadn't discovered it yet and so said no. A suddenly changing circumstance. Or perhaps the investment you counted on for retirement didn't come through. A suddenly changing circumstance. Or you got cancer. When that happens, we think something has gone wrong in the universe. God has made a mistake. It wasn't supposed to happen this way.

Proverbs 16:9 is one of the most profound verses in all the Bible: "The heart of man plans his way, but the LORD establishes his steps." You make your plans, but God determines which way you're going to go. Suppose you say, "I'm going to Bithynia because they need the Gospel," and suppose God wants you instead to go west to Troas. So you try to go to Bithynia, and you are turned away at the border. God says, "I'm going to wash out the road that way, and I'm going to lock the door this way." So even though you wanted to go north, there's nothing that way. You have to go west! That's what happened to Paul.

Please read the next sentence carefully. *What we call circumstances is really the sovereign hand of God in our lives.* The circumstances that come into your life, whether good or bad, have all come down to you from the good and gracious hand of God. They are all ultimately for your benefit and for his glory.

How did Paul decide to go north in the first place? When east was cut off, he had to go north. What made him decide to go west at the end? When the north was cut off, that was all that was left; so he went west and preached the Gospel. That's what I mean by suddenly changing circumstances. *Proverbs 16:9 tells us that didn't happen by chance.* It never does for the people of God. Who is it that opens the doors? It's God! Who is it that shuts the doors? It's God! Who gives opportunities? It's God! Who takes them away? It's God! He is the one who is in charge. Sometimes his will is seen by nothing more profound than suddenly changing circumstances.

There is a third principle we must consider when seeking guidance from God.

Answer #3:
Guidance may come through supernatural events

This happened in Troas. When they got to that seaport town, Paul had a vision of a man from Macedonia standing and begging him, "Come over to Macedonia and help us." Paul was in Troas, which was in Asia; but Macedonia was in Greece—the continent of Europe. In between is the Aegean Sea. What is the significance of the man from Macedonia? *If Paul goes to Macedonia, he's taking the Gospel from one continent to another.* That represents a major, historic expansion for the Christian faith. From the moment Paul stepped on Macedonian soil, Christianity was no longer an "eastern religion."

I have already said that sometimes God does speak supernaturally through dreams, visions, and supernatural signs. I also said it doesn't happen very often. But God can do it. That's what he did here. It was a vision, but the vision was in line with the Great Commission to take the Gospel to the whole world. *This dream was completely compatible with the Word of God and with Paul's previous experience.*

Answer #4:
Guidance comes through wise counsel joined with common sense

Acts 16:10 reveals the final principle of God's guidance: "And when Paul had seen the vision, immediately we sought to go on into Macedonia, concluding that God had called us to preach the gospel to them." The word "concluding" means to discuss the matter with other people, debate the alternatives, figure out the best way to go, and then come to a conclusion. It's a word that implies the strategic use of the mind. It's what happens when you put a puzzle together. You put the pieces together to make it all fit. This particular Greek word was used for taking different colored threads and putting them together to make a beautiful pattern.

Paul, Silas, and Timothy talked it over, discussed everything that had happened—where they had come from, where they couldn't go—and talked about the open door and the vision of the man from Macedonia. When they put it all together, they concluded that God wanted them to go to Macedonia. *That's the final way that guidance comes—through wise counsel and simple, plain, ordinary, garden-variety common sense.*

JUST DO IT!

Notice that once they figured out God's will, they immediately did it. "Immediately we sought to go on into Macedonia." Once you have determined the will of God, what's the next step? Just do it! Once you've figured it out, don't sit around and talk anymore. Get up and do it!

Why were they so quick to do it? Because God had called them to preach the Gospel. He had told them *what* to do, he had told them *how* to do it, and now he told them *where* to do it. But that brings us full circle, back to where we started. Back to the ordinary affairs of life. *The reason they went in the first place was because of obedience in the ordinary.* Because they were so committed to doing God's will, they weren't blown away by a vision; they just fit it into the big picture and said, "Okay, that's where we go." And off they went.

When they went to Macedonia, did they know what was going to happen? Did Paul know in advance who was going to be there to meet him or what the outcome of the trip would be? No! When you decide to do the will of God, will you know in advance what the results will be? No! Why? *Because though God shows us his will, he doesn't show us the future.* What does he show us? The next step! How does God reveal his will to us? Step by step by step!

A PASTOR'S PILGRIMAGE

I have had several chances to put my words into practice. Like most pastors, I have moved more than once. I've already related in the first chapter how the letter came from Texas inviting me to become the first pastor of a brand-new church in a Dallas suburb. As I look back on the decision to go to Dallas, I see God's hand clearly at work, partly by nudging me in the right direction through the inner urging of the Holy Spirit, partly through the advice of friends, and very much through the outworking of the ordinary circumstances of life. Nothing dramatic happened; just a slow unveiling of God's will, one step followed by another by another.

The decision to come to Chicago was quite different. In the first place, I was born and raised in the South. Never had I dreamed of moving to the Midwest. But when the time came to make a decision, I found myself torn between a church in Oak Park, Illinois, and another church in Arizona. After praying and seeking godly counsel, I truly didn't know what to do. I wanted to go to Arizona, but my wife wasn't so sure. My friends were divided—one of them telling me that deep down I was an "Arizona kind of guy." I never got to find out what that meant because for various reasons the church in Arizona interviewed me and then decided to look elsewhere. At the time their decision devastated me. I remember writing God a three-page letter expressing my frustration that he would make such an obvious mistake.

"I THINK YOU SHOULD GO TO CHICAGO"

Meanwhile, the church in Oak Park continued to talk with me. During that period of confusion I traveled to Chicago to preach at Calvary Memorial Church for the first time. There was no problem with that because I knew I was not coming to Chicago. So it was just a fun weekend. Or so I thought. Things went so well that I agreed to return as a candidate—albeit a bit reluctantly. A few days before our trip we got a phone call from a friend who told us, "I think you should go to Chicago."

Still doubting, we traveled to Oak Park for the candidating weekend. The Pulpit Committee put me through twenty-four different meetings, interviews, and services in four days. On Friday night several hundred people gathered in the church dining room to listen as I answered questions from the audience for over two hours. By the time that session was over, I was tired and not feeling very well. The five of us were jammed into a single hotel room. I just wanted to go home to Texas. It was a combination of things—the schedule, the unending questions, the unfamiliar environment, the enormity of the move, and a feeling of extreme exhaustion. That night I hit bottom.

I told my family in very colorful language that under no circumstances were we coming to Oak Park. After I finished, my wife looked at me and said what wives have said to husbands in similar moments since the beginning of time: "Grow up." That was the last thing in the world I wanted to hear. She went on to say that we didn't have to come to Oak Park, that we could go back to Texas and see what God wanted us to do next. Although I wasn't happy to hear that, I couldn't argue with her advice; so I decided to go to bed and sleep on it.

The rest of the weekend seemed to go much better. I also recall that after the Sunday morning service I was meeting with someone in the pastor's office when I heard someone tapping on the window. My middle son Mark (who was then seven years old) had crawled through an open window and was exploring the roof of the church. When I looked up, he grinned at me through the window. It was a portent of things to come. By the time we flew back to Texas, my wife and I both felt that if God wanted us to come, we could do it.

"I Sensed You Were Fighting God's Call"

Three days later the phone rang. It was the same friend who had called us earlier. She told us a strange story. "Last weekend I felt impressed to start praying extra-hard for both of you. The Lord spoke to me, and I sensed that you were fighting his call to

Chicago. So I prayed that you wouldn't fight the Lord, but that you would be open to his will." She told Marlene that she felt led to pray that prayer on Friday and Saturday—the very days when we were struggling so much. There was no way she could have known what we were going through, but God spoke to her, and she prayed for us at the very moment when we needed it. I can't tell you what that did for me. That confirmed what we had already felt—that God wanted us at Calvary.

As I write these words, I am in my fifteenth year as the senior pastor of Calvary Memorial Church. These years have been exciting, turbulent, and unpredictable. They have also been the most fruitful years of my ministry. The question I hear most often these days is, "How long are you going to stay?" The answer is always the same. I have no idea because I never planned to come to Oak Park and I never thought I'd be here this long. The future is as much a mystery to me now as it was when I came here fifteen years ago.

Looking back, I marvel that God could bring a reluctant Jonah like me to the place of his choice. I did everything I could to go to Arizona, but God had other plans. With very little cooperation from me, the Lord patiently guided me step by step from Dallas to Chicago—a journey I would never have made on my own. For that reason I've never doubted that I am exactly where he wants me to be. As I think about this, I am reminded of the gospel song that includes these lines: "He doesn't make you go against your will, he just makes you willing to go." That's my testimony. At every step of the way he led me—sometimes through inner convictions, often through circumstances, sometimes through the advice of friends, sometimes through what seemed to be supernatural confirmation. All of it worked together—just as the Lord promised—to lead me in the path I should follow.

SEVEN CRUCIAL QUESTIONS

That's my story. But every Christian should have a similar story. What God did for me was not unique. God has promised to guide his children, and he will do it. That brings us back to our key text in Acts 16. *Paul was guidable; therefore God guided him.* That's the message of those verses that seem at first to contain no message at all. What happened to Paul will happen to you if you are guidable. I want to close this chapter—and this entire book—with seven questions you ought to ask yourself whenever you are facing a major decision in your life.

1. *Am I in a place of complete guidability?* Are you open to whatever the Lord wants? Or are you so set in your ways that what you're really saying is, "Lord, guide me as long as you tell me to go where I want to go"? Are you willing to do whatever the Lord asks you to do?

2. *Have I studied this issue from every possible angle?* Use your mind. Write down the pros and cons. Make a list. Take notes. Research the question thoroughly. Study the decision from every possible angle. Have you done that?

3. *Have I sought wise counsel?* Many foolish decisions would be avoided if only we would dare to ask advice from others. Have you asked for advice from people who owe you nothing but their honest opinion? Have you discussed this decision with people who have been where you are right now?

4. *Do the circumstances point in one particular direction?* Sometimes God reveals his will by opening one door and closing another. Is there an obvious blockade down one road and an open path down the other? Have your circumstances suddenly changed in some unexpected fashion?

5. *Have I searched the Scriptures in order to discover what God has to say about my decision?* This step must not be skipped. I believe that God's Word will have something to say—directly or

indirectly—about every situation you face. Open your Bible. Read it carefully. Take notes. Underline key passages. Search the Scriptures. Compare one passage with another. Note the commands, the warnings, the many examples. God has something to say to you in his Word. Make sure you give him a chance to say it.

6. *Is there supernatural guidance I should consider?* This won't always happen. But sometimes there will be circumstances that seem to be supernatural movements of God that you ought to bring into consideration.

7. *Am I willing to do God's will without regard to the consequences?* Remember, the will of God has more to do with *who* you are than with *where* you are. God's will is less a matter of geography and more a matter of the heart. Are you willing to do what God wants and then to leave the consequences with him? If the answer to this is yes, you are an excellent candidate to know God's will.

FOCUS ON THE LORD—NOT THE DECISION!

I can imagine one objection you might raise at this point. You could state it many different ways, but it goes something like this: "I've been offered a new job and you haven't told me whether I should take it or not!" "I'm in love with two girls. Should I marry Sally or Beth? Or what about Jill over there? You haven't told me what to do!" "I'm thinking about moving to South Carolina or Minnesota, but Oregon is looking pretty good to me. You haven't told me what I should do."

Yes, I have told you what you should do! Your problem is, you're focusing on the decision, not on the Lord. *When we focus properly on the Lord, the decision will take care of itself.* If we believe in God, we must believe that once we are guidable, he will guide us. If we don't believe that, we might as well give up in our search for God's will.

Let me state this in the form of a long proposition: Once you are open and soft and bendable before the Lord . . . once you are willing to take the next step . . . once you are willing to do God's will . . . at that point you must believe that when you need to make a decision, God will give you whatever wisdom and insight you need *at that moment*, so that whatever decision you make will be his will for your life. You won't have 100 percent certainty, but he will literally guide your thoughts while you are thinking them so that as you are open to him, he will guide you to exactly the place where he wants you to be!

But what if at that point you make a mistake? I believe that if you are truly open before the Lord, truly soft and bendable before him, truly guidable, if for some reason you come to the decision and you make a "mistake," he will overrule that decision in the long run and guide you exactly where he wants you to be for your good and his glory. *If God is God, that must be true.*

When the time comes, make the best decision you can and leave the results with God. This follows from everything else I've shared in this book. When the time to decide comes, when you've thought about it, prayed about it, talked it over, sought godly counsel, researched your options, looked at the circumstances, searched the Scriptures, and waited on the Lord, when you've done everything you know how to do and the moment of truth comes, take a deep breath, close your eyes if you need to, and then go ahead and make the best decision you can make. I've purposely written that as a run-on sentence because it describes how most of our decisions are made. We wait and wait and wait and then we finally decide. And even then we still have to trust the Lord with the results. He's God and we're not. His purposes will stand.

Make your plans. Submit them to God. Be bold when you

need to be bold. Don't be afraid to decide. Leave room for God to change your plans at any time. Then trust God with the results.

I've already said that God wants you to know his will more than you want to know it. Your knowing God's will is his responsibility, not yours. That means it is God's responsibility to show you his will, to guide you in the right path, to give you everything you need, and then to enable you do his will. All you have to do is trust him with the details of your life.

LIFE IS LIKE A ROLL OF THE DICE

Here are two other verses of Scripture we need to consider. Proverbs 16:33 says, "The lot is cast into the lap, but its every decision is from the LORD." Most of us don't understand the concept of casting lots. In the Old Testament, the Jews often used this method to determine God's will. It sometimes involved using different colored balls or rocks, mixing them together, and then seeing which one fell out of the bag first. In that sense casting lots is like rolling dice. *It appears to be a random act of chance.* But God is behind those colored stones. He determines which one falls out of the bag first. This means that there are no accidents in life, no random events, and no such thing as luck. Even seemingly meaningless things fit into his plan. I paraphrase that verse this way: "Life is like a roll of the dice, but God is in charge of how the numbers come up." *Because that is true, you can trust him to give you whatever wisdom you need to make wise decisions and to bring about proper outcomes so that you can do his will every day of your life.*

What's the most important factor? Guidability! "Delight yourself in the LORD, and he will give you the desires of your heart" (Psalm 37:4). As you delight yourself in the Lord, his desires are going to become your desires. You are going to be changed on the inside so that the things you really want are the things God wants for you.

Can you discover God's will for your life? Thank God, the answer is yes! How do you discover God's will? You discover God's will today the same way the people of God have always discovered his will: step by step by step.

God has promised to guide you safely on your journey through this life. You can depend on that. He has said he will be your guide even to the end. He has promised, and he cannot fail. Therefore, I will say it for the last time: *If you are truly willing to do God's will, you will do it!*

QUESTIONS FOR PERSONAL/GROUP STUDY

1. In what sense is discovering God's will our responsibility, and in what sense is it God's responsibility to reveal his will to us?
2. What is guidability, and why is it the single most important ingredient in knowing God's will?
3. When you are seeking God's will for the future, why is it important that you do what you know to be God's will right now? What happens when you disregard this principle?
4. How do you feel about the statement, "when we focus on the Lord, the decision will take care of itself"? Is that a statement of strategy or of priority? Does that mean we shouldn't worry about our decisions at all?
5. When you know the will of God, you are to do it. Period. Why it is important not to delay when God's will has become plain to you?

GOING DEEPER

Let's take another look at the seven crucial questions. Think about several recent decisions you have made, or about a major decision you are about to make. Then rate yourself in each area on a scale from 1 to 5, with 1 being "Not true at all" and 5 being "I am very strong in this area."

1. I truly want the Lord to guide my life. 1 2 3 4 5

2. I have studied this decision from every angle. 1 2 3 4 5

3. I have sought wise counsel from many people. 1 2 3 4 5

4. I have taken changing circumstances into account. 1 2 3 4 5

5. I have studied the Bible carefully, seeking guidance from God for my situation. 1 2 3 4 5

6. I have considered the possibility of supernatural guidance. 1 2 3 4 5

7. I am willing to do God's will without regard to the consequences. 1 2 3 4 5

Now review your list. Does one area stand out as something that needs more attention right now? Make that area a matter of prayer, asking the Lord to give you specific wisdom for the decisions you must make.

If you would like to contact the author, you can reach him in the following ways:

By letter:

Ray Pritchard
Calvary Memorial Church
931 Lake Street
Oak Park, IL 60301

By e-mail: PastorRay@calvarymemorial.com

Via the Internet: www.keepbelieving.com